A SOVIET VIEW
of the
AMERICAN PAST

AN ANNOTATED TRANSLATION OF THE SECTION ON
AMERICAN HISTORY IN THE
GREAT SOVIET ENCYCLOPEDIA
(BOLSHAIA SOVETSKAIA ENTSIKLOPEDIA)

TRANSLATED BY
ANN E. YANKO • PETER A. KERSTEN

EDITED WITH AN INTRODUTION BY
O. LAWRENCE BURNETTE, JR. • WILLIAM CONVERSE HAYGOOD

ANNOTATED BY
WARREN L. WITTRY • MERRILL JENSEN • LEON F. LITWACK
O. LAWRENCE BURNETTE, JR. • FRED HARVEY HARRINGTON

PREFACE BY
ADLAI E. STEVENSON

THE STATE HISTORICAL SOCIETY OF WISCONSIN
Madison • 1960

First published, January, 1960
Portions of this material were published simul-
taneously in the Autumn, 1959, issue of the WIS-
CONSIN MAGAZINE OF HISTORY, *a copyrighted*
quarterly journal of the Society.

Manufactured in the United States of America
[NAP] • I

PREFACE

A TRICKLE of Soviet visitors—let us hope it will become a two-way stream —is beginning to arrive in the United States. They are intelligent people, Soviet musicians, scholars, scientists, managers, and farmers. When they return home we can hope some of them will compare their first-hand impressions here with descriptions of the United States in the so-called *Great Soviet Encyclopaedia.*

Although men tend to see what they have been taught to look for, the contrast between the America these Russians have seen and the account they read in the official reference book may produce some healthy shocks.

Today 800,000,000 people in the Communist world are having drilled into them a concept of America as a land of greed-ridden past, chaotic present, and dubious future. This concept can prove a deeper danger to the United States than Soviet missiles.

Only a small fraction of the voluminous Soviet writings about the United States is readily available to most of us. This is due partly to the language barrier. But it is only recently that we have become interested in what the Soviets think and say about us.

By translating the *Great Soviet Encyclopaedia*'s section on American history, the State Historical Society of Wisconsin has revealed the streaks in the mirror the Soviet historians hold up to the American past. The translation also casts light on the state of contemporary historical scholarship in the USSR. Rewriting history to conform with philosophical preconceptions is hardly a Russian invention. But seldom has such distortion been practiced with so much devotion, or on so sweeping a scale, as by the latter-day disciples of Marx and Lenin.

Rejecting Western scholars' ideals of impartiality and suspended judgment ("bourgeois objectivism" in the Soviet Newspeak), the Soviet historian portrays himself as a scientist, and as an engineer of public attitudes. For him the laws governing man's past and future actions have been scientifically explained and explicitly forecast, largely by Marx, Engels, and Lenin. He is not inhibited by consideration of the sociological, psychological, or even the theological aspects of human behavior which often perplex Western historians. To him all history is economic; all economics Marxian.

The result, as this present document shows, is a curiously dehumanized account of history in which a stereotyped pattern of impersonal force supplants individual effort. The story of human society resembles the story of an ant hill motivated purely by instinct.

The 1958 Summer issue of the *Yale Review* contains a thoughtful analysis of this and several other sections in the *Great Soviet Encyclopaedia* relating to the United States, including the articles on our creative arts, inventions, and our political leaders. It was written by William Benton, publisher of the *Encyclopaedia Britannica*. Like many of us who have visited Russia in recent years, Mr. Benton was impressed by the enormous commitment to education, and by the widespread curiosity about America. When he talked with editors of the Soviet encyclopaedia, and later read what they print about us, he was profoundly disturbed. So am I.

To the millions of Soviet citizens who turn to this encyclopaedia as trustingly as we of the Western world turn to the Britannica, for instance, the portrait of the America they read therein is the only one most of them will ever see.

The closing assessment of recent Soviet-American relations given in the translation which follows is essentially a vehicle for propagating the post-Stalinist doctrine of coexistence. That an encyclopaedia should be so used will strike many American readers as even stranger than the history they will read in the article itself.

In the interest of that mutuality of understanding which the Soviets say they desire—and to which the majority of us subscribe—I urge that Soviet scholars now be encouraged to translate and publish the accounts given by American scholars and American encyclopaedias of the history of the Union of Soviet Socialist Republics.

In making the following document widely available, the State Historical Society of Wisconsin performs a valuable service to American scholarship. It makes an even greater contribution to the nation by bringing to the fore a document that is important to an understanding of our time.

ADLAI E. STEVENSON

CONTENTS

DIRECTORY OF CONTRIBUTORS

ANN E. YANKO, *Graduate Student in English*
University of Wisconsin

PETER A. KERSTEN, *Graduate Student in Slavic Languages*
University of Wisconsin

O. LAWRENCE BURNETTE, JR., *Book Editor*
The State Historical Society of Wisconsin

WILLIAM CONVERSE HAYGOOD, *Editor*
Wisconsin Magazine of History
The State Historical Society of Wisconsin

WARREN L. WITTRY, *Curator of Anthropology*
The State Historical Society of Wisconsin

MERRILL JENSEN, *Professor of History*
University of Wisconsin

LEON F. LITWACK, *Assistant Professor of History*
University of Wisconsin

FRED HARVEY HARRINGTON, *Vice-President and Professor of History*
University of Wisconsin

HON. ADLAI E. STEVENSON
Chicago, Illinois

INTRODUCTION

WHEN William Benton, vice-president of the *Encyclopaedia Britannica*, visited Moscow in 1955 he called at the offices of the *Great Soviet Encyclopedia (Bolshaia Sovetskaia Entsiklopedia)* on Pokrovskii Boulevard. From this meeting of cultural opposite numbers, rare insight into the editorial operations which determine the form and content for published scholarship for the entire Communist world may be gained.

At the time of Benton's visit, this encyclopedic arbiter of ideas for over 800,000,000 people was being directed by a staff headed by Editor-in-chief B. A. Vvedensky, a scholarly radio technician and physicist, and S. I. Viskov, the executive secretary of the editorial board and a specialist in modern history. With disarming candor the editors frankly admitted that the new second edition of their encyclopedia, the first edition having been published during the period 1927–1947, was being constructed in conformity with a Party decree of 1949, and that in the field of history and social movements, the articles were necessarily keyed to Marxism-Leninism. While admittedly under the yoke of politics and censorship, the editors professed to enlist the collective ability of a wide circle of the most eminent Russian authorities. In theory the editorial board is responsible for the selection of individual authors, but in practice the actual choice is made by staff specialists in consultation with institutions of higher learning. Once articles are received from assigned authors, the manuscripts are subjected to "public discussions" before being enshrined in the colossal entombment of all dogma and knowledge as revealed to the disciples of Marx, Lenin, and Stalin. [See Benton's illuminating article, "Great Soviet Encyclopedia," in the *Yale Review*, 47:552–568 (June, 1958).]

The plight of the Soviet historian and encyclopedist who labors under a flexible standard of truth may be graphically demonstrated by the dilemma posed by the liquidation in 1953 of Lavrenti P. Beria, who had been accorded an extensive and fulsome biographical sketch in one of the early volumes of the new edition of the *Bolshaia* [vol. 5, pp. 22–23]. The Encyclopedia, ostensibly in response to the overwhelming demand of its 250,000 subscribers, produced a special section expanding the adjacent articles on F. W. Bergholz (an eighteenth-century courtier), the Bering Sea, and Bishop Berkeley and supplied instructions for scissoring out the Beria sketch and replacing it with the new section. Thus were the offending traitor and his biography flushed down the Orwellian "memory hole."

The year following Benton's visit, volume 39 of the *Bolshaia* was published containing an article on the United States of America [pp. 557 to 654], a section of 97 pages with illustrations. As a section within the general article there appeared a new (revised) sketch of 23 pages on the history of the United States—the most widely available, the most recent, and presumably one of the most definite treatments of American history available in the Soviet Union. In translation, that sketch is here presented. The contributing authors of the historical section were: 1607–1898, M. N. Zakharova, M. M. Malkin, and N. I. Somin; 1898–1917, I. A. Beliavskaia; 1917–1928, A. V. Berezkin; 1929–1941, B. N. Krilov; since 1941, S. I. Viskov, one of the assistant editors of the Encyclopedia. Of the group, only M. M. Malkin had participated in the writing of the earlier article on U. S. history which appeared in the 1945 edition.

Russian historians of America apologize for their difficulty in periodizing their field and for the inadequacy of their research, but their latest effort probably serves their contemporary purposes reasonably well. For Americans it is a curious and highly illuminating combination of information, ignorance, deliberate omissions, and distortions. Decidedly less friendly than the 1945 sketch, it still conforms to the recognizable outlines of American history, and its authors demonstrate a surprising degree of restraint in prostituting their craft. Their work appears to be a serious, professional effort in historical scholarship under the conditions imposed by the Soviet system, and is here accepted as such. Admittedly a highly compressed and elementary interpretation by our standards, American scholars will argue with it for its calculated misrepresentations and for what it chooses to be left unsaid.

Two central themes run through the entirety of the section: A consistent pattern of imperialistic expansionism throughout our history is doggedly constructed, and all instances and repressions of racial, social, and economic unrest are deliberately magnified. The former construction serves as historical documentation to the Russian view of current international problems; the latter magnification attempts to explain why American capitalism has not fallen victim of its own decadence. Once the Marxist lexicon is accorded a liberal transliteration, even the more startling deviations from our own understanding of our past can find some kind of rough substantiation. Within this lexicon, "bourgeoisie" pertains to the middle class or propertied interests and is unfavorably presented wherever possible. The disunity and lethargy of the American "masses" baffles the Soviet historians, and they scorn our "reformist" leaders for actively seeking to cure the excesses of capitalism rather than permitting them to fester into revolution. Realizing the improbability of an American revolution, the Soviets approve of the "progressive" aspects of American life which bring it into closer harmony with the socialist ideal, but avowed Socialists who compromise the theory of the necessity of revolution are guilty of the heinous crime of "sectarianism." The unflattering aspects of our heritage—unrest, predjudice, and injustice—are fully but casually presented. Challengeable interpretations are usually developed within a context of convincing documentation and statistics. The history here presented, while not the crass propaganda of the journalist, is a revealing commentary on Soviet historical scholarship and on the Russian misconceptions of America.

Since the field of history involves the very nub of the ideological struggle between America and Russia, it is important that the Russian historical concept be made generally available. Certainly, it is not required that Americans subscribe to the current Soviet interpretation of their past. But it is of prime importance that an intelligent awareness and sufficient credence be accorded it to gain some understanding of the Soviet reaction to America present. And in the process we may incidentally discover something about ourselves from the fresh viewpoint of critical if prejudiced observers.

The historical scholarship which reposes so self-confidently in the ivy-clad academic towers of the Western world has but a shadowy counterpart in the stark factories of Soviet learning. The name is the same, but the canons, purposes, and fruits are vastly different. Like the science which throws new stars and moons into the firmament, Soviet historiography is harnessed to the service of the State. Indeed, Soviet historiography *is* a science, its practitioners professionally organized as a branch of the Soviet Academy of Science. Differing from the Western art primarily in terms of emphasis, selection, and prejudice, the Soviet science is built upon the ideological concept of "dialectical and historical materialism" and rejects the Western concept of critical or "objective" history, for which it has little understanding and even less patience. Because history, like religion, deals in transcendental truth, in Soviet Russia it has been cut off from its classical roots, fitted with new moral values and concepts, and subjected to a flexible standard of judgment. Soviet historians since the Revolution have labored, according to their own lights and under their own canons, to create a new historical past after each shift in the winds of Party doctrine, skillfully retaining a degree of professional competence and integrity while becoming highly proficient at flushing outmoded truths down the memory hole.

In the relatively brief span of Soviet history, the Russian counterpart of Charles A. Beard, M. N. Pokrovsky, dominated Soviet historiography from 1919 to 1932 and established a school of historical interpretation solely in terms of economic determinism and class warfare. Under his leadership, the study and writing of history in the USSR was abstract and schematic, narrow in scope, unpeopled by living or convincing personalities, and unrelieved by any splashes of local color. It was severely critical of pre-Revolutionary Russia and ignored the history of the external world. By 1936, however, Pokrovsky became a posthumous victim of a new shift in the Party line and his scholarship was degraded as "defeatist, anti-scientific, anti-Marxist, and anti-Leninist." With Pokrovsky's decline came a resurgence of Soviet historical scholarship. In 1931 the discipline, hitherto largely ignored in the Soviet curriculum, was re-established as an independent study in the elementary schools; in 1934 a government decree laid down elaborate and systematic principles for the teaching of national history; in 1936 the study of foreign history was reintroduced in the higher educational institutions.

The revival of Russian historiography also embraced a revival of interest in the history of the Western world—especially that of the United States. Since the language barrier and ideological roadblocks have limited the Soviet's utilization of standard American scholarship, the sketches in the two editions of the *Great Soviet Encyclopedia* must be consulted to trace the course of that revival.

The first edition of the *Bolshaia* was published irregularly from 1927 to 1947 in sixty-five volumes under the general editorship of N. I. Bukharin, V. V. Kuibyshev, and others. Thoroughly Soviet in treatment yet international in scope, it carried signed articles by the presumably best-qualified specialists, provided extensive bibliographies, and appeared under the sanction of the State. The volume containing the general article on the United States was published in 1945; it occupied 263 pages (as against 97 in the later edition) and contained a section devoted to history. Generally written in a friendly vein, the high lights of American history were identified as the Revolution and the Civil War, both ending in "progressive" victories, although "bourgeois elements" subsequently capitalized upon them. Woodrow Wilson was presented as a "liberal statesman," and the American intervention in Russia in 1918–1919 was not mentioned. The Russian historians could find no elements of a genuine class struggle in American history prior to the 1920's, but they did express sympathy for the suffering of the depression which they charged to capitalistic excesses, and they were generally sympathetic toward the relief and reform efforts of President Franklin D. Roosevelt.

The article was published in the twilight of Soviet-American wartime solidarity, and almost immediately after its publication, sketch and encyclopedia ran afoul the new policy of hostility toward the West, cultural isolation, and the new crusade against "cosmopolitanism," i.e., the corrupting consequences of wartime cultural associations with the external world. The result was a reinterpretation of history, and the sharpening of it as a weapon against the enemies of international Communism.

Since 1945 Soviet historians have been busily rewriting history to fit the new conditions of the world. Previous condemnations of czarist expansionism are now justified as positive goods and precedents for contemporary expansionist designs. The United States having emerged as the primary threat to Soviet policies, all references to wartime solidarity were replaced by the bare bones of chronology of the global aspects of the war. The formerly admired experiment in democracy and humanitarianism became the first of a long list of Russian bogies, justifying domestic restrictions and privations and serving as a spur to overtake the material greatness of the enemy. In Russian propaganda America was described as culturally decadent, dominated by undefined "ruling circles," prostrate at the feet of Wall Street, the last citadel of dying imperialism, the enslaver of the world, and the destroyer of culture. Under the immediate supervision of the Department of Propaganda and Agitation of the Central Committee of the All-Union Communist Party (Agitprop, for short), the new history was fashioned and the degree of political censorship tightened to prevent the correcting influence of external and objective truth. The Soviet intelligentsia and propaganda organs were directed to stamp out "cosmopolitanism" and "bourgeois objectivism." In 1949 the Party directed the publication of the new, second edition of the *Great Soviet*

Encyclopedia, to serve the new purposes of anti-cosmopolitanism and anti-Americanism. It was directed to "show with conviction and in full the superiority of socialist culture over the decadent culture of the capitalist world," to "expose imperialist aggression and apply Party criticism to contemporary bourgeois movements in the realms of science, technology, and culture," and to be "saturated with Bolshevik Party spirit." [*Pravda,* March 26, 1949.]

The intensification of the Cold War witnessed an even greater effort to erase the favorable image of America in the Soviet Union. The trend of anti-Americanism and the use of historical forms for propaganda purposes probably reached a climax with the publication in 1949 of *Here She Is—America!* under the imprint of the Young Communist League. Ostensibly a compilation of travel impressions by Russians in the United States, the work viciously misrepresented contemporary America as a land of poverty, hunger, and unemployment, in which marching throngs of homeless cried for bread.

Beginning in 1950, a monumental effort was undertaken to minimize the contributions of the Western Allies to final victory over the Axis Powers, not to say attribution to the Allies of a large measure of guilt for precipitating the war. American and British imperialists, it was claimed, instigated Hitler's perfidious attack on Russia for the purpose of encouraging mutual destruction. Once Russia showed unexpected strength in resisting, the West made common cause but did not carry out its commitments. The Korean conflict placed a new burden upon Soviet historians to discredit America historically. Taking their cue from the current charges of germ warfare in Korea, a 1952 tabulation, unchallenged—if not produced—by Soviet historians, concluded that "the immense majority of the 144 wars [presumably counting all Indian skirmishes] which the USA has waged in its history were barbarian, inhuman and exterminational wars against defenseless or poorly-armed nations" [quoted in W. W. Kulski, *The Soviet Regime; Communism in Practice* (Syracuse, 1954), 18–19.]

The death of Stalin in 1953 had a tremendous effect upon all levels and areas of Soviet intelligentsia. There was an immediate relaxation of the rigors of anti-comopolitanism, of the excesses of cultural isolation, and of the more severe forms of political censorship. But years of conditioned response are not lightly sloughed off. Soviet historians continued to thunder at their American colleagues for being tools of monopolistic capitalism and imperialism, for supporting an unscientific historical criticism, and for denying the objective existence of history. [E. B. Cherniak, in *Voprosy Istorii (Problems of History)* 1955, (6):179–186, as reported in *Historical Abstracts,* 1:2493.] At the same time, they castigated themselves for their previous isolation and for failing to provide themselves with sufficient documentary material and secondary works on the Western world [unsigned articles in *Voprosy Istorii* 1954 (7):3–12; 1954 (4):177–182; and 1956 (1):3–12, as reported in *Historical Abstracts,* vols. 1, 2].

In the rehabilitation of Soviet historiography in the post-Stalin era the elimination of the "cult of the individual" has resulted in history of greater balance and scope, and Soviet historians have exhibited a new interest in the "progressive aspects" of American history. Clearly with official sanction, Soviet historians were incensed when a wave of anti-American bias went so far as to call Benjamin Franklin a "troubadour of American middle-class dreams of world conquest"; in revulsion they wrote three articles in praise of him. Stalin's own *History of the Great Patriotic War* was assailed for its attempts to hide defeats and deflate the global nature of the conflict. But Soviet historiography was not liberated in the fall of Stalin. It has shed an old orthodoxy for a new, in which independence of conclusions and freedom to express them are still absent or unexercised. Soviet historiography still turns on the principles of rigid mechanistic causation and inflexible inevitability, producing history which is often superficial, overly simplified, dogmatic, and downright false by the canons of Western scholarship. Soviet historiography has yet to produce its definitive history of the United States and presumably follows, as we do, its encyclopedia material as an outline of interpretation.

As a contribution toward seeing ourselves as seen by our Soviet viewers through however small a peephole in the colossal wall which divides us, the present translation into English has been made, annotated to counter or correct the more glaring misstatements or gross misinterpretations, and is here presented. If some small insight into the difficulties of mutual understanding are derived, the effort will have been worth while. The translation has been kept purposefully as literal as possible to eliminate the chance of misconstruing shades of meaning and to preserve the flavor of the Russian. Liberties have been taken only in paragraphing and punctuation to facilitate an easier reading of the English text. Points of cross reference (*q.v.*) have been included in the text in order to indicate those events and individuals which the Soviet editors deem worthy of more detailed treatment elsewhere.

The editors are deeply indebted to a host of individuals for making this community undertaking a reality. The translators and annotators have given selflessly of their time and talents. Colleagues on the staff of the Society and in the departments of History and Slavic Languages at the University of Wisconsin have supplied invaluable advice and criticism. The personal interest and encouragement of the distinguished contributor of the Preface has sustained a hope that a larger purpose than idle curiosity may be served. Most particularly, the enthusiastic support of the Director of the Society has been indispensable.

O. L. B., Jr.
W. C. H.

THE PRE-COLONIAL ERA

annotated by WARREN L. WITTRY

THE TERRITORY of the USA before European colonization was inhabited by Indians and Eskimos. The Indians belonged to an Americanoid race which derived from the Mongoloid. It is assumed that the ancestors of the Indians migrated to America from northeastern Asia, across the region of the Bering Straits, from ten to fifteen thousand years ago.[1]

The Indians and Eskimos of North America were found in various levels of a primitive-communal order. The Eskimos inhabited the Arctic shore of North America from Alaska to Greenland. Their main occupation was hunting, on sea and on land. There are preserved in the social system of the Eskimos faint vestiges of the "generation" system of social order.[2] On the western coast of North America, Indian tribes (Tlingit, Haida, and others) combined fishing with hunting. Social relationships were characterized by the presence of patriarchal dominance, of the development of barter, and of property inequality. In the Southwest the most developed were agricultural tribes called Pueblo Indians (K'eres, Hopi, Zuni, and others). They used irrigation in agriculture, built large communal houses,[3] knew the art of pottery to a higher degree than the other Indians of the North American tribes, and carried on an active trade with neighboring tribes. By the time of European colonization, the Pueblo Indians were found in a state of transition towards a paternal generation.

Nomadic tribes inhabited the prairie region, their main occupation having been the hunting of grassland animals, especially the bison. It is assumed that having settled in the prairie, these formerly agricultural tribes completely adapted their way of life to a nomadic form. Many prairie tribes had, simultaneously with a matriarchal line, the beginnings of a patriarchal generation. The prairie Indians formed a number of war alliances, of which the biggest and strongest was the family union of the Dakota tribes. Californian Indians were behind the other North American tribes in their level of development. They obtained a livelihood by gathering wild fruits, particularly acorns, which they cultivated by a rather complex method; in addition, they engaged in fishing and hunting. In the eastern part of the continent there lived agricultural tribes: Iroquois, Algonquins, Muskogy, and others. According to examples of tabulation by American historians, in the sixteenth century about one million Indians populated the territory of the United States.[4]

---

[1] This was the estimated time generally accepted until the late 1940's. Since then, radiocarbon dating has established the presence of man in North America as early as 30,000 years ago.

[2] The unilateral evolutionary concepts of Henry Lewis Morgan (1818–1881), an American anthropologist, were endorsed by Marx and Engels and are still prevalent in Soviet anthropology, although they have undergone profound modification in modern anthropology in the Western world. According to Morgan's theory, societies went through evolutionary stages from simple to complex. While the rate of advancement might vary, nevertheless all societies had to go through the same stages.

[3] Pueblos of the Southwestern United States were not and are not communal in the communistic sense. They consist of juxtaposed apartments.

[4] A. L. Kroeber, in his *Cultural and Natural Areas of Native North America* (Berkeley, 1947), estimates the Indian population of North America, north of Mexico, to have been 1,025,950.

THE COLONIAL PERIOD AND THE AMERICAN REVOLUTION

annotated by MERRILL JENSEN

Colonial Period: 1607–1775

SHORTLY AFTER the discovery of America by C. Columbus (1492), English expeditions led by John Cabot discovered Newfoundland, the northeastern peninsula of America, and a large part of the eastern coast of North America (down to the 38°).[1] In the sixteenth century the colonization of North America was begun by Europeans. Spain, France, England, the Netherlands, and Sweden carried out the colonization. The Indians offered heroic resistance against the colonists, but the Europeans possessed a huge superiority in weapons; in addition to this, the Indian tribes were disunited and fought among themselves, which also facilitated the conquest of North America by the Europeans. The process of colonization was attended by uninterrupted wars with the Indians (the first war in 1622–1634), the seizing of their land, driving them back to the West, and annihilating them. The first permanent English settlements were founded in the South (in the territory of Virginia in 1607) and in the North (in the territory of Massachusetts in 1620). Having established during the seventeenth and eighteenth centuries a series of colonies (the last in Georgia in 1733) and having seized the Dutch colony of New Netherlands as a result of the war with Holland in 1672–1674,[2] England spread its domain on the Atlantic Coast. As a result of the Seven Years' War, 1756–1763, England seized Canada and Eastern Louisiana, which had previously belonged to France.[3]

In the eighteenth century the Russians explored and began to colonize Alaska (*q.v.*). In the beginning of the nineteenth century Russian settlements sprang up in California.[4]

The English colonies had the greatest development. In the thirteen English colonies founded in the territory of the USA, immigration was mainly from Great Britain and Ireland. Among the immigrants, destitute peasants and artisans predominated. A capitalistic structure began to develop in the colonies. The preference for a small-farm economy spread. For the colonies there were the typical availability of uncultivated land and the severe shortage of manual laborers. The colonists had the opportunity of acquiring sections of land and of establishing independent agricultural communities. Gradually there developed, in combination with the small-farm economy, a domestic industry. In the colonies of New England (*q.v.*) and in the central colonies in the second half of the seventeenth century capi-

---

[1] Although the English "right" to colonize was based on John Cabot's first voyage in 1497, no one knows what he discovered and he disappeared on a second voyage the next year.

[2] New Amsterdam was taken by the English in 1664 and renamed New York. The Dutch recaptured it in 1673 but held it only until 1674.

[3] Britain also acquired East and West Florida from Spain in 1763, as well as several French islands in the West Indies.

[4] Since Russia had only a few forts in California, and never seriously tried to seize the territory from Spain, it is highly exaggerated to say that Russian "settlements sprang up."

talistic manufacturing began to develop.[5] In land ownership there existed several feudalistic elements: the right of primogeniture and entail; in several colonies (for example, in New York) there existed large-scale land-ownership of a semi-feudal type —in which lands were worked by hereditary farmer-tenants paying a fixed rent. Small-scale farmers carried on a struggle against colonial authorities for land and political rights. There occurred many agitations and uprisings in Maryland (in the period 1654–1689); in Virginia (under the leadership of N. Bacon, 1676); in Pennsylvania (1763); in New York (1766); the insurrection of the "Levelers"[6] in North Carolina (1765–1766); and others. Uprisings of the artisans and of the petty urban bourgeoisie took place in Boston (1689); in New York (1689–1691).[7] In the popular movements the "white slaves" took an active part. These were "temporarily indentured servants" (for four to seven years)—immigrants, persons convicted for vagrancy, for political reasons, as well as criminal offenders and colonists who were committed into slavery for unpaid debts.[8]

In the South the slavery of Negroes, first introduced into Virginia from Africa in the beginning of the seventeenth century by Dutch slave traders, was widespread. The slave labor of the Negroes served as a basis for the development in the southern colonies of a plantation economy, the principal crop of which was tobacco until the end of the eighteenth century, and after that cotton.[9] The Negroes, subjected to cruel exploitation and deprived of all rights, stirred up rebellions and sometimes joined together with the "white slaves" or the Indians.[10]

In the area of the economic development of the colonies, tensions grew between them and the mother country. The colonies' growing bourgeoisie competed successfully with English merchants in the fur trade with the Indians, in fishing, in shipbuilding, and in trade with the West Indies. England impeded the economic development of the colonies, trying to keep them as a source of raw materials and as a commodity market for her own industry. England especially hindered the commercial ties of the colonies with other countries. A law of 1750 prohibited construction in the colonies of blast furnaces, rolling mills, and iron foundries. However, despite this, industry in the colonies developed. The trade among the colonies grew, as well as their trade with the West Indies, especially during the Seven Years' War, 1756–1763 (q.v.). It was difficult for England in this period to counteract the economic development of the colonies. With the development of capitalism, the gradual decline of a single market, and the strengthening of economic ties among the colonies, the bourgeoisie of the North American people was formed.

After the Seven Years' War, England undertook drastic measures in order to arrest the further economic development of the

---

[5] If private ownership is meant by "capitalistic manufacturing," the use of the term is accurate. There was a steady growth in the number of artisans who "manufactured" in homes and small shops, but aside from the iron industry, there was no large-scale industry in any latter-day sense.

[6] The common name for the troubles in North Carolina, both then and since then, is the "Regulator Movement," although occasionally opponents of it sometimes spoke of the people involved as "levelers."

[7] The revolts in 1689 in the colonies followed the Revolution of 1688–1689 in England. They were carried on by the political leaders of the colonies who were not, on the whole—compared to their fellow colonials—"petty urban bourgeoisie."

[8] "White slaves" has a vastly different connotation in America today. The proper name is "indentured servants." The categories listed here do not include the vast majority of indentured servants who were simply Europeans too poor to pay their passage to America and who voluntarily signed contracts to work out their passage money.

[9] Indigo and rice were the two other basic southern crops, although tobacco always ranked first in value.

[10] Marxist historians have placed much emphasis on Negro revolts, but there was perhaps only one of any consequence. Furthermore, there is no evidence that the "white slaves" ever joined with the Negroes. The important fact was that the whites, particularly in South Carolina, were always afraid that the slaves would revolt.

colonies. In 1763 a royal proclamation was issued prohibiting settlement of the land beyond the Allegheny Mountains. The campaign directed against contraband trade grew stronger. Trying to conceal from the colonial population the huge expenses incurred in the Seven Years' War,[11] the mother country resorted to taxation of the colonies. In 1765 a stamp duty was levied, constituting the first attempt at direct taxation of the colonists. In 1765 the mother country undertook an attempt to quarter English soldiers in the colonies.[12]

A significant role in the liberation movement against the mother country belonged to an organization formed in 1765, "The Sons of Liberty," consisting of artisans, laborers, farmers, and merchants, and led mainly by radical representatives of the bourgeoisie. Meeting in New York the assembly of representatives of the colonies was of great importance in their unification. The Congress determined the boycotting of English commodities.[13] A powerful popular movement forced England to retract the Stamp Tax in 1766,[14] but the English Parliament at the same time confirmed the mother country's right to issue any laws in regard to the colonies. In 1767 taxes on the importation by the colonies of tea, glass, and paint were introduced.[15] In all the colonies the movement for the boycott of

English commodities and the agitation for the development of local manufacture grew stronger. In 1770 the taxes on commodities were lifted, except for a small tax on tea. The quartering of English soldiers in the colonies led to a bloody clash between the colonies and the troops in Boston in 1770. In 1772 in Boston, and after that in other cities, Committees of Correspondence were founded, taking into their own hands the leadership in strengthening the national liberation struggle against the mother country. The leadership of the Committees of Correspondence belonged to the bourgeoisie, but representatives of the artisans, of the petty urban bourgeoisie, and of the farmers were also members of them.

In December 1773 the members of the organization "Sons of Liberty" threw into the sea a shipment to Boston of a load of tea belonging to the English West Indies Company[16] (the Boston Tea Party). The English government launched repressions: in 1774 the Boston harbor was closed. New contingents of soldiers were directed to Boston, which was declared in a state of siege. These measures and the annexation to Canada through the Quebec Act of 1774 of the vast North American territory beyond the Alleghenies[17] provoked a new upsurge of the revolutionary movement, including various strata of farmers rushing to settle in the rich western lands. In 1774 the First Continental Congress (q.v.) was organized, adopting the resolution on the boycott of English trade and on the necessity of resisting the repressions on the part of the English. The English king declaring the colonies rebellious, the colonies were subjected to a blockade.

[11] Instead of concealing the public debt, England argued openly that it had been contracted to defend the colonies, and that therefore the colonies should help pay a portion of the expense of the British army in America during the post-war years. The colonial newspapers contain accurate accounts of the English debt and the debate over the problems created by it.

[12] The decision to leave British troops in America was made before the end of 1762 and troops were in the colonies constantly thereafter.

[13] The Stamp Act Congress is the proper name for this meeting. The Congress did not decide to boycott English goods. This was done later by merchants and politicians in some of the northern cities.

[14] The pressure of British capitalists, merchants and manufacturers hard hit by depression and declining trade with America, had more to do with the repeal of the Stamp Act than a "powerful popular movement."

[15] Paper was also included in the Revenue Act of 1767.

[16] The reference here is to the East India Company.

[17] Only the region northwest of the Ohio River was added to Quebec.

The War for Independence 1775–1783

IN 1775 the American people began the Revolutionary War (q.v.) for independence from England. In April, 1775, farmers defeated the English troops near Concord and Lexington. In March, 1776, American soldiers occupied Boston. On the Fourth of July, 1776, the Second Continental Congress in Philadelphia adopted the draft by Thomas Jefferson (q.v.) of the Declaration of Independence. The Declaration being revolutionary in character, it proclaimed the formation of an independent state—the United States of America.

At the head of the army, formed from partisan detachments and the colonial militia, Congress as far back as 1775 had placed G. Washington. In the first years of the war the English, having received substantial reinforcements from England, succeeded in winning a series of battles. English soldiers occupied New York (1776) and Philadelphia (1777). The turning point in the course of the war occurred after that, as American soldiers won the major victory of Saratoga (October, 1777). After the serious defeat of Yorktown (October, 1781), the main forces of the English surrendered to the Americans.

The international situation was favorable for the USA and was conducive to victory, being characterized by the intensification of the conflict between England and other European states. In 1778 a Franco-American military alliance was signed, which the activities of the USA's representative, B. Franklin (q.v.), helped to conclude. The French army and navy took part in the war against England. In 1779 Spain entered the war against England; in 1782, Holland.[18] Also important to the colonial victory was the position of Russia, on whose initiative (Declaration of 1780) a number of European states declared an "armed neutrality," directed against England. In 1783 the Versailles Peace Treaty was signed,[19] by which England recognized the independence of the United States.

The War for Independence was a bourgeois revolution. Popular masses won the victory over England, playing a decisive role in the revolutionary war against England. The Negroes took an active part in the struggle against the English.[20] As a result of the War for Independence the American people freed themselves from the colonial oppression hampering the development of productive powers. Royal lands and a large part of the property belonging to the Loyalists (q.v.) were confiscated, slavery in the northern states was abolished, the Church was separated from the State, and suffrage was somewhat extended. Conditions for the rise in the northern USA of the capitalistic way of development in agriculture were created by the earlier elimination of the existing elements of feudalism in land ownership and by the nationalization in 1787 of lands in the West.[21] At the same time, under the influence of the industrial revolution in England and of the increasing demand for cotton by the English textile industry, in the South of the country a slave-holding economy was established. With the transition of the plantations to the growing of cotton, slavery—as K. Marx pointed out—changed into a commercial system of exploitation. The southern USA became the source of raw materials for the English textile industry.

K. Marx and F. Engels rated highly the historical significance of the Revolutionary War for Independence in North America and emphasized that it exerted a great influence on the development of the struggle against the feudal-absolutist order in Europe. V. I. Lenin considered the War for Independence one of the great, really liberating, really revolutionary wars.

---

[18] England declared war on Holland in 1780.

[19] This was a "Treaty of Paris," not Versailles.

[20] The writer seems to be somewhat confused about his own terminology. In Marxist theory a "bourgeois" and a "mass" revolution are not the same thing. It is false to say that the Negroes took an active part in the Revolution. Some few did but the great mass did not.

[21] The correct date is 1784.

FROM THE REVOLUTION
THROUGH RECONSTRUCTION

annotated by LEON F. LITWACK

The economic and political development of the USA at the end of the eighteenth and in the nineteenth centuries (to the beginning of the Civil War)

AS A RESULT of the War for Independence the bourgeoisie and the planters came into power in the country, turning the victory over England to their own class interests. Following the war the economic dislocation weighed heavily on the shoulders of the workers.[1] The intensification of the class struggle manifested itself in the postwar period in the agitations in the Army (1783) and the uprisings of the poorer farmers (1786–1787; Shays' Rebellion, *q.v.*), suppressed by armed strength.[2] The revolt of the farmers reinforced the aim of the bourgeoisie towards the consolidation of their dictatorship and the centralization of power for the suppression of popular mass resistance.

Put into effect in 1781, a constitution—"The Articles of Confederation"—formulating a union which preserved the sovereignty of the independent states, did not insure the unity of the country. The right of taxation remained with the states, and separate customs laws for each state were preserved, which impeded the development of a common national market. Representatives of the ruling classes at the Constitutional Convention in Philadelphia in 1787 drew up a new federal constitution, consolidating the rule of the bourgeoisie and of the planters in the form of a bourgeois democracy.[3] Congress assumed the right of taxing and regulating trade among the states, and of the disposal by means of a nationalized reserve of the uncultivated lands in the West. More powers were given to the President. The Constitution sanctioned the existence of

---

[1] Economic dislocation also affected the bourgeoisie and, to a lesser extent, the planters. New England merchants and shipowners had freed themselves from the mercantilist acts of trade, but they now found themselves excluded from any commercial privileges in the British Empire. American manufacturers who had expanded their operations during the war now faced stiff British competition. But the resourceful shipowners and merchants managed to find new outlets for their trade. By 1786, without the benefit of the Constitution, the United States was well on its way toward economic recovery.

[2] Under the leadership of Daniel Shays, an ex-Revolutionary War officer, farmers in western Massachusetts staged an armed rebellion in protest against low prices for their products, high taxes, frequent foreclosures, and an unsympathetic eastern-dominated state government. As news of the rebellion spread elsewhere, conservatives deplored the lack of a strong central government which could deal effectively with such challenges to the propertied interests.

[3] Charles Beard, in *An Economic Interpretation of the Constitution*, contends that holders of federal and state bonds, merchants, manufacturers, creditors, land speculators, and slaveholders played a dominant role in drafting the Constitution, and that these interested groups derived important economic advantages from the establishment of the new government. Forrest McDonald, in *We the People*, recently attempts with questionable success, to refute Beard's conclusions and to demonstrate that every geographical region, as well as every economic and political interest, had representatives at Philadelphia.

slavery in the South.[4] The Constitution, put into effect in 1789, displeased the workers. Part of the bourgeoisie and the planters also protested against it. Under the pressure of the development in the country of a widespread movement, in 1791 the first ten amendments to the Constitution were added, confirming the bourgeois-democratic freedoms. These amendments received the name of the Bill of Rights.

In the process of a sharp political struggle in 1789–1791 in the USA, the bourgeois parties of the Federalists and the Republicans were formed. The Federalists voiced the interests of the large-scale mercantile bourgeoisie, the large landowners of the North, and part of the planters of the South.[5] They advocated the strengthening of the power of the federal government. The Republicans (or Anti-Federalists), supporting the democratization of the Constitution, relied in that period on a bloc mixed in social composition, consisting of part of the bourgeoisie, small and medium-scale planters, farmers, and petty urban bourgeoisie. The Republicans were supporters of the preservation of States' rights.[6] Unlike the Federalists, patterning their behavior after England, the Republicans came out in support of Revolutionary France.

The commander-in-chief of the Colonial Army during the War for Independence,

G. Washington (q.v.), became the first President of the USA (1789–1797). In 1793 Washington declared the neutrality of the USA in the war of the coalition of European states against Revolutionary France. In 1794 the government concluded a treaty with England, degrading for the national sovereignty of the USA (Jay Treaty, q.v.), which stirred up widespread resentment in the country.[7] Opposition also sprang up in connection with the course of the government's domestic policy, which to a significant degree was formed by the adversary of democracy and leader of the Federalist Party, A. Hamilton, Secretary of the Treasury in 1789–1795. The taxation policy of the government particularly provoked the farmers' resentment, which led to the revolt of the farmers of Pennsylvania in 1794 (known in bourgeois literature by the name of the "Whiskey Rebellion") and to the agitations of the farmers of Pennsylvania in 1799.[8] The Federalist J. Adams (President,

---

[4] Actually, the Constitution carefully avoided the words "slave" and "slavery" and left the matter to the states for determination. However, the Constitution did provide that representation and direct taxation be apportioned among the states on the basis of the number of "free persons" and three-fifths "of all other persons;" that Congress in 1808 might prohibit the immigration of certain persons (directed at the foreign slave trade); and that the states must return escaped persons "held to service or labour" in other states.

[5] The bulk of Southern planters objected to Alexander Hamilton's financial program and aligned themselves with Thomas Jefferson's Republican Party. Hamilton's program, it was feared, would sacrifice agrarian interests in favor of the eastern speculative-moneyed-industrial interests. In the absence of a comprehensive study of the political attitudes and affiliations of early American workers, any conclusions regarding them along these lines can only be conjecture.

[6] Once in power, however, a majority of Republicans abandoned some of their constitutional scruples and displayed a willingness to construe the Constitution liberally whenever it served their best interests. The Federalists, on the other hand, moved into a strict States' rights position.

[7] The most "degrading" aspects of Jay's Treaty arose from its failure to deal with the violation of neutral rights and impressment, and its limited and negligible trade concessions. Nevertheless, Great Britain did agree to evacuate the posts she had maintained in the Northwest, in return for a pledge that the United States government would assume the debts owed by American citizens to British subjects. Southern planters objected to the latter provision, inasmuch as Great Britain refused to consider Southern claims against England for slaves abducted and damage inflicted during the Revolutionary War.

[8] Upon Alexander Hamilton's suggestion, Congress in 1791 imposed an excise tax on distilled spirits. Trans-Appalachian farmers, especially those in Pennsylvania, objected to such "discriminatory" legislation. In the absence of good roads on which to transport their bulky goods to Eastern markets, many of these farmers turned their corn and rye into whiskey and transported it to nearby cities and towns. This constituted a valuable source of hard money with which to purchase supplies. Armed resistance to the tax collectors broke out in 1794, only to be suppressed by an army headed by President George Washington, General Henry Lee, and Alexander Hamilton. Out

1797–1801) passed the law "against aliens," directed against revolutionary immigrants from France and Ireland, and the law "against sedition," threatening imprisonment for criticism of government actions.[9]

The relations of the USA with France became sharply strained. The policy of the government met with the opposition of the democratic classes, uniting with the Republicans.[10] This assured victory in the presidential elections for the leader of the Republicans, T. Jefferson (President, 1801–1809). Jefferson's administration repealed the reactionary laws of 1798 and instituted a series of progressive reforms;[11] in particular, an agrarian law was passed (1804) reducing the size of land sections for sale from government land reserves in the West to 160 acres, together with the lowering of selling prices and installment payments. The agrarian policy of the Republicans contributed to the settlement of western lands by the farmers. The acquisition in 1803 from France of western Louisiana for fifteen million dollars substantially extended the territory of the USA. The establishment of diplomatic relations between the USA and Russia in 1808–1809 contributed to the strengthening of the USA's international position.

England continued to remain the principal adversary of the USA in the beginning of the nineteenth century. Taking advantage of the USA's economic dependence on England and of its military weakness, the English bourgeoisie continued to seek reestablishment of its dominion in the former colonies in North America. In a violation of the Versailles [Paris] Peace Treaty of 1783, England, during a long period did not withdraw her troops from the Northwest forts, and seized American merchant ships.[12] In response to these actions, the retaliatory embargo (the prohibition of trade with European countries and the closing of the ports of the USA to foreign ships) provoked resentment of the bourgeoisie, unwilling to lose trade profits. In 1809 the embargo was lifted by Jefferson, before the end of his term as President.[13] The relations between England, who still was not reconciled to the loss of her North American colonies, and the USA became still more strained. The English Navy continued to seize American ships.[14]

In June, 1812, the USA declared war on England. In this war the American Army

---

of 150 arrested, two obscure farmers were convicted, sentenced to death, and subsequently pardoned by Washington.

[9] Congress passed the Alien and Sedition Acts in 1798. The Sedition Act resulted in the prosecution of twenty-five persons and the conviction of ten Republican editors and printers. President Thomas Jefferson subsequently pardoned all those convicted under the act, and Congress restored the fines with interest.

[10] The division of opinion was not quite this clear-cut. French interference with American ships and commerce, the much-publicized XYZ Affair, and the ill-treatment of American envoys in France aroused a great deal of public anger, even among the "democratic classes" and the Republicans. Actually, the policy of the Adams Administration successfully thwarted the Federalist "warmongers" and led to a settlement with France.

[11] The "reactionary laws" undoubtedly refer to the Alien and Sedition Acts. Rather than repealing these laws, the Jefferson Administration allowed them to expire. But the Republican Congress did repeal all internal taxes, including the excise tax on distilled spirits, and the Federalist Judiciary Act. This completed the "series of progressive reforms." The Jefferson Administration did not tamper with the Hamiltonian system of banking and finance. In fact, the Republican Party now attracted to its ranks men of substantial liquid as well as landed capital.

[12] By Jay's Treaty (1794), Great Britain agreed to evacuate the Northwest forts by June 1, 1796.

[13] The Non-Intercourse Act, signed by Jefferson prior to leaving office, repealed the Embargo Act and reopened trade with all nations except France and Great Britain. The President could resume trade with either nation as soon as one of them agreed to a recognition of neutral rights.

[14] This is an inadequate explanation of the causes of the War of 1812. In addition to Great Britain's alleged desire to recover her North American colonies, it is important to consider the aspirations of agrarian imperialism, a resumption of Indian troubles, and, perhaps most important of all, the Western and Southern demand for "an open market for the productions of our soil now perishing in our hands because the mistress of the ocean has forbid us to carry them to any foreign nation."

suffered a series of defeats. American troops attempted to invade the territory of Canada, but failed. In 1814 the English occupied the capital of the USA, Washington, and burned a large part of the city. Nevertheless, during the course of the war, the American Army and Navy, chiefly privateers, succeeded in delivering a series of blows to the English on land and sea. In January, 1815 (by this time after the signing of a peace treaty), the Americans smashed the English troops near New Orleans.[15] The USA remained in accord with the peace treaty concluded in Ghent in December, 1814, until the Border War.[16] A result of the war was the strong independence of the USA. After the Anglo-American war, 1812–1814, the international status of the USA became stronger.

In 1819 the USA forced Spain to sell to it Florida, which previously had been virtually seized by the USA.[17] In 1823 the President of the USA, J. Monroe, proclaimed a doctrine which at that time was directed against the intervention of European States in the affairs of the Western Hemisphere; at the same time the expansionist tendencies of the USA in regard to the Latin American countries were reflected in it even then.

The availability in the USA of extensive lands and natural resources, the widespread immigration to the USA from Europe and the influx of foreign capital, as well as the weakness of the USA's neighbors, created, with the strengthening of the capitalistic attitude, favorable conditions for the swift economic development of the country. However, the USA remained in economic dependence on England. In view of the increasing demand for cotton as a result of the advances of the industrial revolution in England and of the industrial revolution in the Northeast of the USA beginning in the nineteenth century, the development of a plantation economy in the Southern states, based on the widespread use of slave labor, increased. The cotton was exported mainly to England, from whom industrial products were imported. The planters strove to seize the new lands in the West—a condition of the existence of slavery, as under a plantation economy the soil quickly becomes exhausted. Settlement of the lands in the West was accompanied by continuous wars with the Indians and attended by their extermination.[18]

The economic development of the USA went in two directions—industrial-agricultural in the North, and slave-owning in the South—which became the source of sharp social conflicts and was accompanied by a tense political struggle within the country. The bourgeoisie were in agreement with the planters.[19] In 1820 there was some expansion in the area of slavery (to 36° 30′); at the same time slavery was prohibited in

---

[15] In the absence of modern trans-Atlantic communications, news had not yet reached New Orleans—or the East—that the Peace of Ghent had ended the war. However, Andrew Jackson's victory so enhanced American prestige abroad and at home that few regretted the battle had been fought.

[16] The Treaty of Ghent provided for a peace without victory. Neither side made any substantial concession. No mention was made of neutral rights, impressment, or interference with American commerce. The "Border War" or "Aroostock War" was fought over the correct location of the Maine-Canadian boundary. However, the Webster-Ashburton Treaty of 1842 settled this bloodless conflict as well as other outstanding differences between the United States and Great Britain.

[17] The United States unilaterally annexed West Florida in 1810, justifying it on the basis of the Louisiana Purchase. Nine years later, the Adams-Onis Treaty ceded East Florida to the United States. Andrew Jackson had laid the basis for such a cession by his 1818 foray into East Florida to suppress hostile Indians and eliminate a refuge for runaway slaves. The ease with which Jackson marched through Florida revealed the weakness of Spanish authority there and virtually forced Spain either to sell the territory or face an arbitrary seizure.

[18] By 1840, most of the area east of the Mississippi had been cleared of Indians. Those who resisted the move westward faced extermination.

[19] Actually, the Panic of 1819 accelerated the break between Southern planters and a large portion of the Northern bourgeoisie. By the time of the Missouri controversy, many Northerners asso-

the territory north of 36° 30′ (Missouri Compromise, q.v.). Fear of the power of the popular masses united the planters and the bourgeoisie.[20] Several sections of the bourgeoisie were also closely connected economically with slavery.[21] This explained the policy of compromise on the part of the bourgeoisie, its indecision, and its inconsistency in the struggle against slavery. However, the compromises, not eliminating the conflict between the Northern capitalists and the Southern slaveowners, were able only to postpone their inevitable clash.

In the North industry developed comparatively quickly, and in the West, agriculture. By the end of the 1820's, the building of railroads began, which particularly encouraged the rapid development of the West. Settlement of the West extended the domestic market and hastened the development of industry. The industrial bourgeoisie was concerned with the protection of industry from foreign competition and sought the establishment of high protective tariffs on industrial goods. But the planters protested against high tariffs. The farmers were also concerned with the repeal of high tariffs.[22] The Tariff of 1828, introduced by the ad-

ministration of John Quincy Adams (President, 1825-1829), provoked especially fierce resentment.[23]

A circumstance of the aggravation of the political conflict between the bourgeoisie and the slaveowners was the disintegration of the old Republican Party. A new political party sprang up. In 1828 the Democratic Party was formed, which united in the beginning period part of the planters, part of the bourgeoisie connected with the Southern slaveowners, and also a substantial part of the farmers. In 1834 the Whig Party was formed, representing the interests of the upper bourgeoisie.[24] In the presidential election of 1828, the candidate of the Democratic Party, A. Jackson, won (President, 1829–1837). Jackson pursued a policy of exterminating the Indians and became a supporter of slavery.[25] At the same time, under pressure by the popular masses in the period of his presidency, several reforms were effected. White men in almost all states were given the right of suffrage; the law of imprisonment for debts was revoked; and

---

ciated Congressional rejection of beneficial economic legislation with Southern power in government and thus opposed the admission of a new slave state. Northern humanitarian opposition to slavery and its expansion was also increasingly manifest.

[20] John C. Calhoun hoped to utilize such a fear to unite the planters and the bourgeoisie, but he failed. A capitalist-planter alliance, Calhoun contended, could effectively deal with any proletarian or abolitionist challenges to the established order and would thus successfully prevent the impending outbreak of a class war. However, such an alliance based on States' rights and nullification did not conform to the economic interests of antebellum Northern capitalism. Daniel Webster made this quite clear during the Nullification Controversy. For a discussion of Calhoun's proposed coalition, see Richard Current, "John C. Calhoun, Philosopher of Reaction," in The Antioch Review, (Summer, 1943), 223-234.

[21] By 1830, New York merchants had developed a profitable triangular trade with the cotton South, commercial New York, and industrial England. Moreover, Northern businessmen assumed control of much of the South's commercial activity.

[22] As far as can be determined, Northwestern farmers supported high tariffs. Henry Clay's "home market" argument greatly appealed to these farmers. High tariffs would create urban and industrial centers in the East, which would in turn create additional markets for Western farm products.

[23] The Adams Administration bears little or no responsibility for the Tariff of 1828 (also referred to as the Tariff of Abominations). Jacksonians dominated the House committee which reported the bill. Indeed, the sole Adams member denounced the work of the committee. Adams signed the final act but held Congress completely responsible.

[24] It is exceedingly difficult to equate economic interests with a particular political party. This can be said of American political parties in virtually any period. Both the Democrats and the Whigs attracted to their ranks groups of Americans from all sections and all social and economic strata.

[25] President Jackson did accelerate the Indian removal policy of his predecessors. On the subject of slavery, Jackson had always deplored any agitation that might prompt slaves to revolt, and as President he agreed with the efforts of members of his administration to ban abolitionist literature from the mails. Jackson himself was a substantial holder of slaves.

the existence of labor organizations, which until then had been prohibited, was permitted.[26] Workers formed local parties in Philadelphia and New York (1828–1829), and then in a number of other cities.[27] The workers' parties demanded free distribution to all who wanted land; abolishment of debtors' prisons; the institution of democratic reforms; and the reduction of the working day to ten hours. However, these few weak workers' parties were disintegrating by the beginning of the 1830's.

In the beginning of the thirties in the USA a mass movement, abolitionism (q.v.), developed widely, advocating the abolition of Negro Slavery.[28] The abolitionists developed an active propaganda against slavery. Their principal organ was the newspaper, *Liberator* (1831–1865), of which the abolitionist W. L. Garrison became the editor. By 1840 the members of the abolitionist societies numbered nearly 200,000.[29] One of the main factors in the struggle with slavery was the numerous uprisings and rallies of the Negroes, the most significant of which was the uprising under the leadership of Nat Turner in Virginia (1831).

The planters brutally suppressed the actions of the Negroes and prosecuted the abolitionists, resorting largely to the Lynch court.[30] With the 1840's, the political conflict in the country became even more intense. In 1840 the abolitionist "Party of Freedom" was formed.[31] In 1848 the popular farmers' party, the Free Soilers (q.v.), which the labor organizations supported, was formed. The party stood for the prohibiting of the further extension of slavery in the territory of the USA, and against the expansion of the slaveholders.[32] In the forties the socialist movement, in which socialist-utopians predominated, grew stronger (Owenists, Fourierites, and others).

The population of the North, especially where the wave of immigrants from Europe settled, increased more rapidly than in the South. By 1860 there were twenty-two million people in the North, in the South (according to approximate calculations) nine million, of which Negro slaves constituted about four million. However, the Democratic Party, changing in the forties to the party of the Southern planters and uniting with them part of the banking and merchant bourgeoisie, succeeded in encouraging abuse and demagogy to keep power almost all the time until 1860.[33]

Attempting to gain new lands, the slaveowners in 1836 worked for the secession of Texas, where slavery began to be extended, from Mexico. In 1845 Texas was annexed

---

[26] In *Commonwealth v. Hunt* (1842), Chief Justice Lemuel Shaw of Massachusetts upheld the legality of trade unions and collective bargaining. However, the decision enjoined labor organizations to pursue their ends by "honorable and lawful means," and thereby gave unsympathetic courts substantial room for anti-union action.

[27] The working class origins and nature of these political parties varied greatly in time and area. In several cases, bourgeois reformers and politicians captured control of the organizations. See Edward Pessen, "The Workingmen's Movement of the Jacksonian Era," in the *Mississippi Valley Historical Review*, 43:428–443 (December, 1956), and Joseph Dorfman, "The Jackson Wage Earner Thesis," in the *American Historical Review*, 54:296–306 (January, 1949).

[28] This requires a definition of "a mass movement." Militant abolitionism did develop in the 1830's, but it attracted relatively few members to its ranks. Nevertheless, the abolitionists did constitute a very vocal minority and undoubtedly helped to influence anti-slavery sentiment in the North.

[29] This is a greatly exaggerated membership figure. In the 1840 election, for example, the presidential candidate of the anti-slavery Liberty Party polled only 7,059 votes.

[30] Following the suppression of the Nat Turner uprising, Virginia whites turned on both innocent and guilty bondsmen, tortured and murdered some, transported other "suspects" out of the state, and relegated a few to the courts for disposition. The rebellion also prompted Southern States to tighten their control over slaves, free Negroes, and abolitionist agitation.

[31] The correct name is the Liberty Party.

[32] The Free Soil Party not only called for an end to slavery expansion but demanded a federal homestead act which would give small farms to persons who intended to settle on the public domain. This point appealed to farmers and to a number of Eastern workingmen.

[33] The Democratic Party also included in its ranks large numbers of workers and farmers.

to the USA by a one-sided act.[34] As a result of the Mexican War in 1846–1848 (q.v.), the USA, under the peace treaty of Guadalupe–Hidalgo (1848), took almost half of all the territory of Mexico. According to the treaty of 1853 (called the "Gadsden Treaty" for the name signed to the treaty the USA sent to Mexico) the USA cut off still more from Mexico—about 140 square kilometers of territory.[35] As a result of the settlement of a dispute with England (1846), the USA seized part of the territory of Oregon.[36] The USA tried to buy or seize the island of Cuba, which belonged to Spain. It tried to impose its influence on Nicaragua and other countries of Central America. In 1850 the USA concluded an agreement with England on the question of control over the future canal across the territory of Central America (Clayton–Bulwer Treaty, 1850, q.v.).[37] In the forties the expansion of the USA spread to China. In 1844 the USA pressed an unjust treaty on China in Wanghia. The USA participated in the suppression of a popular uprising in Taiping, 1851–1864.[38] Threatening with

armed force, it compelled Japan in 1854 to conclude an unjust treaty.[39] In 1858 the USA forced China to sign a one-sided agreement.[40] The interests of the slaveowners and of part of the bourgeoisie coincided in the matter of expansionist foreign policy, but several groups of the bourgeoisie, concerned with the restriction of slavery, protested against the seizure of Texas, against the war with Mexico, and against interference in the affairs of Central America.

In the middle of the nineteenth century, slavery hampered even more the development of productive strength in the country and the growth of industry. However, the clashes between the bourgeoisie and the slaveowners usually ended in a compromise. After a long debate in Congress in 1850, California was admitted into the Union as a non-slaveholding state. But as a result of the agreement of the bourgeoisie with the slaveowners, who were taking advantage of their predominant influence in the government and Congress of the USA, Congress in 1850 passed a law concerning fugitive slaves, under which the authorities in the Northern states were obliged to catch the runaway slaves.[41] In 1854 the planters succeeded in passing the Kansas–Nebraska Act (q.v.), in accordance with which the

---

[34] Texas appeared to be quite content with this "one-sided act." She was admitted to the Union as a state, rather than as a territory; she would have to agree to the formation of any additional states from her territory; and she retained her public lands, but had to pay the debts incurred by the previous Republic.

[35] James Gadsden, a prominent Southern railroad official, negotiated this treaty in order to clear the way for the construction of a Pacific railroad along the most practicable route. Mexico agreed to sell the coveted area for the sum of $15,000,000 (later reduced to $10,000,000).

[36] American citizens had already settled in Oregon. The United States annexed the territory in a treaty with Great Britain which established the 49th parallel as the boundary between the United States and Canada (1846).

[37] The United States and Great Britain agreed never to obtain or exercise exclusive control over an isthmian ship canal, or to fortify it. Such a canal, if constructed, would be neutral and open to both nations on an equal basis. This agreement remained in effect until abrogated by the Hay-Pauncefote Treaty (1901).

[38] By the Treaty of Wanghia, the United States secured an equal right to exploit Chinese markets and the right of American citizens accused of

crimes in China, other than trade infractions, to be tried before an American consular officer. In the Taiping Rebellion (1851–1864), the United States threw its influence behind the existing regime but took no active military measures in suppressing the civil war.

[39] Backed by an impressive display of American naval strength, Commodore Matthew C. Perry forced Japan to open some of her ports to American commerce.

[40] By the Treaty of Tientsin, the United States secured privileges recently won through armed intervention by Great Britain and France. A subsequent agreement, the Burlingame Treaty of 1868, clarified American rights in China and guaranteed unrestricted Chinese immigration to the United States.

[41] The Fugitive Slave Act of 1850 strengthened previous legislation and gave to the federal government virtually unlimited power to apprehend runaway slaves. The alleged fugitive had no recourse to common legal safeguards, such as a jury trial and a judicial hearing. The act also subjected

question of slavery in the territories was to be decided by the settlers themselves.[42] By these decisions the border agreed on between the free and the slaveholding states, established in 1820 at 36° 30′, was erased. In the interests of the slaveowners, the Supreme Court of the USA in 1857 handed down a decision on the matter of the Negro, D. Scott (*q.v.*), ruling that slavery could exist in any state.[43] All of these measures brought about an intensification of the abolitionist movement. In 1854–1856 the clashes between the farmers and the slaveowners who had settled in Kansas broke out into an armed struggle. In this conflict the government supported the slaveowners.

In 1854 the bourgeois Republican Party was formed. The Free Soilers came into it, constituting its left, radical-democratic wing. The farmers and workers supported the party's left wing. The right, moderate-liberal wing of the party consisted of representatives of part of the bourgeoisie (mainly industrial), concerned with the development of a domestic market and with trying to restrict the extension of slavery.

As a result of the economic crisis of 1857 and following that, an extended depression, the condition of the farmers and workers became worse. In the fifties the workers' movement became even more organized: the number of strikes increased; trade unions grew. Gradually the workers were drawn into the political conflict. The struggle of the workers merged with the struggle of the farmers for land and against slavery.[44] A radical current grew stronger among the abolitionists. The Negroes took an active part in the struggle against slavery. F. Douglass, an eminent representative of the Negro people and an important figure of the American revolutionary movement, played a prominent role in the fight for the freedom of the Negroes.[45] By means of a "secret railroad" having its own stations (the homes of citizens, sympathizing with the fugitives), Negro slaves, fleeing from the Southern states got over into the North, usually to Canada. The armed

---

anyone concealing or rescuing fugitives to fine, imprisonment, and civil damages. However, Northern Negro resistance—sometimes violent—and the actions of several Northern communities and states virtually nullified the operation of the law.

[42] Senator Stephen A. Douglas of Illinois introduced the Kansas-Nebraska Bill and secured a sufficient number of Northern and Southern votes to insure passage. Historians have debated Douglas' motives. He had presidential aspirations and needed Southern support for his nomination; he had real estate which might increase in value with the construction of a central transcontinental railroad; and he had consistently championed the cause of railroad expansion. An argument frequently used against the central route for a transcontinental railroad was that it would have to cross unorganized Indian country. But the Kansas-Nebraska Bill would overcome this objection.

[43] Chief Justice Roger B. Taney ruled, in effect, that only a state could abolish slavery within its own territory. Congress could not prohibit slavery in the territories, and, therefore, the Missouri Compromise had always been null and void. Moreover, Negroes, whether free or slave, were not citizens of the United States and could not claim any of the rights and privileges of citizenship.

[44] Marxist historians have generally given much more credit to working-class anti-slavery agitation than the facts would seem to substantiate. The working-class movement was by no means united on the subject of slavery although it undoubtedly opposed the further expansion of that institution. While some unions and labor leaders expressed anti-slavery sentiments, large numbers of American workers feared the competition of emancipated slaves and vigorously opposed the abolitionist movement. The Republican Party appealed to workers and farmers because of its stand on slavery expansion and its support of a federal homestead act. But the Republican Party repeatedly declared its allegiance to the principles of white supremacy. Indeed, most farmers and workers would probably have agreed with the sentiment of this Ohio Republican leader: "The 'negro question,' as we understand it, is a *white man's question*, the question of the right of free white laborers to the soil of the territories. It is not to be crushed or retarded by shouting 'Sambo' at us. We have no Sambo in our platform. . . . We object to Sambo. We don't want him about. We insist that he shall not be forced upon us." Quoted in Earl B. Wiley, " 'Governor' John Greiner and Chase's Bid for the Presidency in 1860," in the *Ohio State Archaeological and Historical Quarterly*, 58:261–262. (1949).

[45] If the term "American revolutionary movement" connotes the ante-bellum struggle of Negroes for equal rights, Frederick Douglass' role has been correctly assessed.

revolt led by John Brown (*q.v.*) which occurred in 1859 was suppressed, but it became a stimulus for strengthening the struggle of the Negro slaves and the workers and the farmers against slavery. The dissatisfaction of the popular masses—of the Negroes and of the poor white population of the South—grew even stronger.[46] The presidential elections of 1860 took on the character of a keen battle for power. The planters tried to surmount a crisis of the plantation economy by taking new lands and by the forced diffusion of slavery in the whole territory of the USA.[47] For this they sought, at any price, to keep federal power in their hands. After the presidential elections, in which the candidate of the Republican Party, A. Lincoln (*q.v.*) won (President, 1861–1865), the slaveowners, long preparing revolt, reached a decision on the secession of the Southern states. In February, 1861, the creation of a slaveholding confederacy was announced. The slavery of Negroes was declared to be their "natural condition."[48]

[46] Although Negroes and poor Southern whites possessed many common grievances, it must not be inferred that they acted together to correct these abuses. Southern poor whites had been carefully indoctrinated in the supremacy of the white race, and, in their depressed economic and social status, tenaciously held to this one vestige of distinction.

[47] Southern planters did, indeed, encourage the admission of Kansas as a slave state. But no other overt attempts were made at this time to add new lands or force the diffusion of slavery in other parts of the United States.

[48] In view of the great interest expressed by Karl Marx and Frederick Engels in the American Civil War, it is surprising that this general account of United States history gives so little attention to the fundamental causes of that conflict. The Encyclopedia's separate article on the Civil War pays more attention to the economic nature of the sectional struggle and relies in large part on the often perceptive observations of Karl Marx and Frederick Engels, in their *The Civil War in the United States* (New York, 1937). "The present struggle between the South and North," Marx wrote, " is . . . nothing but a struggle between two social systems, between the system of slavery and the system of free labor. The struggle has broken out because the two systems can no longer live peacefully side by side on the North American continent. It can only be ended by the victory of one system or the other." (p. 81).

The Civil War in the USA and the Reconstruction of the South

IN APRIL, 1861, the Civil War (*q.v.*), began. The governments of England and France actively helped the rebels, supplied them with weapons, and endeavored to organize intervention.[49] Also at that time Russia, declining an Anglo-French proposal to intervene in the Civil War on the side of the rebels, took up a position favorable for the Lincoln Administration. The arrival in the USA in 1863 of two Russian naval squadrons, combined with the aggravation of Anglo-Russian antagonisms, helped strengthen the international position of the Lincoln Administration.[50] Part of the bourgeoisie of the North followed an indecisive policy and did not wish to wage the war with revolutionary methods.[51] The North

[49] The English and French governments neither materially aided nor recognized the independence of the Confederate government. The South relied heavily and mistakenly on "King Cotton" to secure foreign recognition, assistance, and intervention. However, the abundance of cotton on the English market in the early years of the war, the development of new sources, and heavy investments in Northern industry, railroads, and state securities helped to insure English neutrality. France was in no position to risk a war with the United States.

[50] Strategic rather than moral considerations appear to have prompted a Russian fleet to visit New York and San Francisco in 1863. Because of an impending war with England, Russia hoped to get its fleet out of the Baltic and into more distant waters where it could prey on British commerce. Whatever the motive, the Russian visit did apparently strengthen Lincoln's international position. Actually, the section devoted to the Civil War implies the two-sided nature of the Russian expedition. "The arrival in 1862 of two Russian squadrons in San Francisco and New York, combined with the aggravation of Anglo-Russian conflicts, *took on the character* of a demonstration in favor of the Northern states." [Annotator's italics.] See F. A. Golder, "The Russian Fleet and the Civil War," in the *American Historical Review*, 20:801–812 (1915).

[51] The frequent reference to the employment of "revolutionary methods" in waging the war should be clarified. Marx's reports on the conflict often complained of the absence of "revolutionary methods," and cited in particular the need for conscription, positive financial legislation, a unified military command, more aggressive military action, and—most important of all—the abolition

was not prepared for war. All this was the reason for Northern losses in the first period of the war (1861–1862) and for the prolongation of it for four years, despite the North's enormous superiority in strength over the South.

Broad masses of workers and farmers, standing against slavery and for democracy and the preservation of the union of the country, were the main force opposing the rebels.[52] After a series of Northern defeats, the Lincoln Administration, under pressure by the popular masses and the radical-democratic wing of the Republican Party, introduced a series of measures bringing about the turning point in the course of the war. In May, 1862, a compulsory draft was announced.[53] At the same time, a law was passed concerning land allotments, according to which every citizen of the USA (or any person arriving in the USA and announcing his desire to adopt American citizenship), by paying a small registration fee could obtain for use a section of land of 160 acres (Homestead Act, q.v.). A purge of traitors in the army and in the state ma-

chinery was carried out.[54] In 1864, General U. Grant, who showed great military skill, became commander-in-chief of the Northern armies. On January 1, 1863, an act was put into effect concerning the emancipation, without land, of the Negro slaves belonging to the planters—participants in the rebellion.[55] Almost 190,000 former slaves poured into the Union Army from the area of the South occupied by the North.[56] Negroes, participating in the struggle with the slaveowners not only on the front but also in the rear of the rebel lines, played a prominent role in achieving the victory. The Negro people made a decisive contribution in the matter of their own liberation in the struggle against the slaveowners. The transition to revolutionary methods of waging war in the second period of the Civil War (1863–1865) insured the complete defeat of the rebels. The victory of the North encouraged the struggle of the workers of the European countries, beginning with the English proletariat, who were protesting against the schemes of Anglo-French intervention.[57] K. Marx and F. Engels carried on an active fight against the threat of intervention.[58]

---

of slavery and employment of Negro troops. Marx attributed Northern failure to adopt such methods to the appeasement of the "loyal" slaveholders of the border states and incompetent military leadership. "In the end," Marx predicted in August, 1862, "the North will make war seriously, adopt revolutionary methods and throw over the domination of the border slave statesmen. A single Negro regiment would have a remarkable effect on Southern nerves." See Marx and Engels, *Civil War in the United States*, 81, 251–253.

[52] The contributions of workers and farmers to the Northern prosecution of the war should in no way be minimized. However, it might be added that Northern workers also helped to swell the ranks of antidraft and anti-Negro mobs. In New York City, for example, mobs made up in part of disgruntled workers and Irish-Americans rioted for four days in 1863 and pillaged and terrorized the Negro section. For the origins and nature of these riots, see Philip S. Foner, *History of the Labor Movement in the United States* (New York, 1947).

[53] Congress passed the Conscription Act on March 3, 1863. All males, 20 to 45, were subject to military service unless they provided a substitute or paid a $300 commutation fee. Actually, the draft provided only a small portion of the Union Army.

[54] The "purge" probably refers to the changes in army command, the arrest of several officers on charges of treason, and the imprisonment or banishment of real and suspected Copperheads.

[55] The Emancipation Proclamation applied only to slaves in areas still in rebellion, thus excluding regions already under federal military occupation.

[56] The estimated number of Negroes in the Union Army varies from 186,017 to 220,000. Of these, about 40,000 came from the border slave states and 93,346 from the seceded states.

[57] On several occasions, English workers demonstrated against the threat of British intervention in the Civil War and expressed their sympathy with the Northern cause. Marx and Engels reported these meetings and credited the English working class with a decisive influence on British neutrality. Frank L. Owsley, in *King Cotton Diplomacy* (Chicago, 1931), cites some pro-Southern as well as pro-Northern English working-class meetings and attributes them in large part to the work of professional political propagandists. In view of the property qualifications for voting, Owsley further questions any influence such meetings might have had on the British government.

[58] In addition to their reports on the political aspects of the Civil War, Marx and Engels fol-

European revolutionaries took a large part in the war of the North against the slave-owners.

The Civil War in the USA, ending in the victory of the North, had, especially in its second stage (1863–1865), the character of a bourgeois-democratic revolution. Peoples' masses carried on a just war against slavery. K. Marx and F. Engels repeatedly emphasized the enormous progressive significance of the Northern fight. V. I. Lenin later noted the progressive and revolutionary character of the Civil War.[59]

The Civil War led to the realization of a series of bourgeois-democratic reforms, creating favorable conditions for the development of capitalism in the country.[60] Conditions were created for the later transformation of the USA to a centralized, unified state. The American way of the development of capitalism prevailed in agriculture. Democratic solutions to the questions of lands in the West and of the freeing of the slaves promoted the expansion of a domestic market.

The defeat of the Southern slaveowners brought before the bourgeoisie of the North the problems of political and economic reconstruction of the South. In the period of the Reconstruction of the South (1865–1877), influential circles of the bourgeoisie, whose interests were voiced by A. Johnson, President of the USA in 1865–1869, feared the intensification and deepening of the revolutionary movement, and pursued a conciliatory policy in regard to the planters.[61] This gave the planters, who were trying to preserve the half-slave position of the Negroes and to keep them from political activity, the opportunity in 1865–1866 to put into effect the anti-Negro "Black codes," and to form terrorist organizations—the Ku Klux Klan and others.[62] Freed from slavery but having received no land, the Negroes found themselves in a half-slave economic dependence on the planters; they were forced to become tenant farmers. The planters, consolidating their position in the South, began anew to enter a claim on the leadership in the government of the country.

Radical Republicans, who had represented the interests of the revolutionary groups of the bourgeoisie, advocated the execution in the South of bourgeois-democratic reforms. Under the initiative of Radical Republicans, Congress passed the Thirteenth, Fourteenth, and Fifteenth amendments to the Constitution (put into effect in 1865, 1868, and 1870, respectively), which made official through legislative channels the abolition of Negro slavery and granted them civil and political rights.[63]

---

lowed the military action with great interest. They severely criticized General McClellan's strategy and urged, instead, that the Union Army make a direct thrust into Georgia which would cut the Confederacy in two and cripple its war effort. The Encyclopedia's separate section on the Civil War credits Marx and Engels with suggesting the strategy which the Union Army adopted successfully two years later.

[59] Vladimir I. Lenin referred to the American Civil War as "world-historic, progressive, and revolutionary" in *A Letter to American Workers* (New York, 1935).

[60] For example, the Morrill Tariff (1861), the Homestead Act (1862), the Pacific Railroad Act (1862), and the establishment of a national banking system (1863 and 1864).

[61] Andrew Johnson, a Jacksonian Democrat, championed the cause of the Southern white yeoman farmer. As an anti-secessionist from Tennessee, he at first impressed the Radical Republicans with his desire to destroy the power of the Southern planter aristocracy. Even Marx wrote to Engels on May 1, 1865, that "Johnson is stern, inflexible, revengeful and as a former poor white has a deadly hatred of the oligarchy." But the Radicals soon learned that Johnson equally detested Republican economic legislation and that his class background dictated a policy of political, economic, and social subordination for the Negro. Indeed, Johnson's avowed enemy, the planter aristocracy, soon became his chief ally and supporter, while most "influential circles of the bourgeoisie" went over to the Radicals, helped to direct Radical Reconstruction along conservative lines, and finally abandoned the Negro to local and state white jurisdiction.

[62] Other "terrorist organizations" included the Knights of the White Camellia, the White Brotherhood, the Pale Faces, the Constitutional Union Guards, and numerous local groups.

[63] The Fourteenth Amendment failed to secure civil and political rights for Negroes, but it did help to secure corporations against discriminatory state legislation. As the amendment was later in-

Having received a majority in Congress, the Radical Republicans, led by Ch. Sumner and T. Stevens, carried out, over President Johnson's veto, laws for the "Reconstruction of the South." The most important of these was the First Reconstruction Act passed on March 2, 1867. According to this law the Southern states were divided into military districts, a military dictatorship was introduced into the South, and former participants in the rebellion, trying to restore slavery and openly opposing the ratified amendments to the Constitution, were deprived of political rights.[64]

The events of the Reconstruction period were revolutionary in character. In the period of the Reconstruction of the South, Negroes and poor whites took a most active part in the political life and, in particular, in the affairs of the newly created administrations of the Southern states, called the Reconstruction administrations; for the first time in the history of the USA several Negro representatives were elected to Congress.[65] This had great progressive significance. Negroes organized the so-called Union Leagues, in which detachments of Negro militia and Negro rifle clubs were formed.[66] These leagues, becoming organizations of a political nature, led the Negroes' armed opposition to the terrorism of the planters and played an important role in the Negroes' struggle for land. In many places Negroes seized sections of land.[67] The Negroes demanded a division of the large plantations in the Southern states. However, the overwhelming majority of the bourgeois representatives of the North was against these demands, condemning thus the very revolutionary reforms to failure.[68]

The victory in the Civil War was won by widespread peoples' masses; but chiefly the upper bourgeoisie, seeking a compromise with the planters, profited by its fruits. By 1872 former rebels received political rights.[69] In the beginning of the 1870's a split occurred in the Republican Party; a substantial part of the Republican representatives protested against continuing the

---

[67] In an effort to achieve economic independence, many Southern Negroes leased, purchased, or pre-empted confiscated and abandoned lands. The federal government at least momentarily encouraged the settlement of Negroes on these lands. In 1864, for example, the federal government settled seventy-five Negro families on a large tract of abandoned land in Mississippi, embracing nearly six ante-bellum plantations. The settlers quickly developed into independent and self-supporting farmers and within a year had repaid the government for its assistance and expenses. In the second year, however, the land was returned to the original owners and the Negroes expelled.

[68] Representative Thaddeus Stevens of Pennsylvania proposed that 394,000,000 acres of land belonging to ex-Confederate leaders (affecting about 10 per cent of the population) be confiscated, that 40,000,000 acres be granted in lots of 40 acres to every adult male freedman, and that the remaining acres be sold and the proceeds applied to the national debt, veterans' pensions, and restitution for war damage to the property of Southern and Northern loyalists. Congress, however, fearing that any confiscation act might set a dangerous precedent, generally expressed little concern for the economic future of the Southern Negro, and thus defeated Stevens' efforts to give the emancipated slave a firm economic basis for his newly won freedom and political rights.

[69] In May, 1872, Congress passed the Amnesty Bill which restored political rights to most Southerners. Indeed, only about 500 ex-Confederate leaders remained unaffected. Passed in an election year, the bill strengthened the Democratic Party in the South and accelerated the overthrow of Radical Reconstruction.

---

terpreted, no state was to deprive any person *or corporation* of life, liberty, or property without due process of law. The Fifteenth Amendment failed to secure equal voting rights for Southern Negroes.

[64] The First Reconstruction Act disqualified from participation in the new state governments and electorate those who had held state or federal positions pursuant to supporting the Confederacy.

[65] State Constitutional conventions met throughout the South in 1867 and 1868. Negroes participated actively in these conventions and in the subsequently established state governments and helped to draft some long-overdue governmental and social reforms. In no state, however, did they actually dominate the government. Two Negroes served in the United States Senate and twenty in the House of Representatives.

[66] Northerners organized the Union League in 1862 to mobilize support for the war. The Radical Republicans captured control of the organization, expanded its operations into the South, and welcomed Negro members. In several areas, Negroes organized League branches, militia units, and rifle clubs.

Reconstruction of the South. In 1877, in conditions which had become strained in the North in the class war of the seventies, an agreement known as the Tilden-Hayes Compromise was effected between the bourgeoisie of the North and the former slave-owners of the South.[70] In the presidency of R. Hayes, the military dictatorship in the South was completely abolished. The Northern bourgeoisie, having betrayed their wartime associates, entered into an agreement with Southern planters aimed at suppressing the movements of the working class, the farmers, and the Negro people. The agrarian question in the South remained unsettled. The bourgeoisie, putting into effect a policy of compromise in regard to the planters of the South, attempted "to re-establish all possible, to do all possible and impossible for the most shameful and base oppression of the Negroes." (V. I. Lenin, *Works*, 4th ed., vol. 22, p. 13.)

The sections of land taken over by the Negroes were almost everywhere taken away.[71] With the help of intimidation and violence, of the organization of Lynch courts and bloody massacres, the Negroes were deprived of virtually all rights. The unjust position of the Negroes was fixed by a series of racist laws later passed in the Southern states.[72] Racial discrimination in regard to Mexicans and immigrants from Asian countries was also preserved in this way. Indians, confined to reservations, did not receive any kind of rights, even formally.[73]

In connection with the inflation beginning in the period of the Civil War, as well as speculation and the development of high prices, the living standard of workers and laboring farmers declined sharply. The stratification of the farmers gained strength, and their dependence on banks grew. The majority of farmers who had received lands in accordance with the Homestead Act were quickly ruined. Their lands were seized by joint-stock companies and banks.[74] The bourgeoisie laid the burden of the huge government debt (over $2,800,000,000) on the shoulders of the workers. The class struggle was intensified, so that it made its manifestation in the strengthening of workers' and farmers' movements. In 1865 a league was formed for the struggle for an eight-hour working day.[75] In 1866 the National Workers' Union (which existed until the begin-

---

[70] Through deaths, retirements, and shifts in political fortunes, the Old Radical Republican leaders disappeared from the scene. In their place arose a new set of Republican leaders—professional political bosses bent on consolidating and institutionalizing Republican rule.
In the disputed presidential election of 1876, the Republicans secured Southern support for the election of Rutherford B. Hayes by assuring the new industrial-minded, Whiggish ruling class of the South that federal troops would be withdrawn, that a cabinet post would go to a Southerner, and that Republican Congressmen would support generous internal improvements, especially railroad land grants, for the South. The withdrawal of troops, coincident with the use of force and violence against the Reconstruction governments and the Negro population, ended Radical Reconstruction and relegated the Negro to an inferior political, social, and economic position. See C. Vann Woodward, *Reunion and Reaction: the Compromise of 1877 and the End of Reconstruction* (Boston, 1951).
[71] Presidential pardons and amnesty restored much of the abandoned and confiscated land to the original owners.

[72] In the last two decades of the nineteenth century, the Southern state legislatures disfranchised the Negro and systematized the old extra-legal code of segregation through the passage of "Jim Crow" laws.
[73] The publication of Helen Hunt Jackson's *A Century of Dishonor* (1881) and the subsequent organization of the Indian Rights Association helped to arouse at least a concern for the plight of the Indian and prompted Congress to adopt some allegedly remedial legislation. The Dawes Act of 1887 dissolved the Indian tribes as legal entities and provided for the division of the tribal lands among the individual members.
[74] The extent of this distress varied in time and place. Farmers generally blamed it on steadily declining prices for their products, exorbitant railroad and grain elevator rates, increasing dependence on crop liens in the South and farm mortgages in the West, high interest rates on loans, and a rigid currency.
[75] By 1868, state-wide organizations, usually called Grand Eight-Hour Leagues, could be found in Illinois, Indiana, Michigan, and Iowa, and a Central Eight-Hour League was organized in New York City.

ning of the seventies) was organized under the leadership of Sylvis (*q.v.*).[76] Socialist influence became stronger.

As far back as the 1850's the Communist Club of New York had been organized. In 1887 in the USA sections of the First Internationale appeared.[77] Marxist ideas were being diffused. In 1867 the farm organization, the "Grangers" (members of the "National Society for the Promotion of Agriculture"), appeared.[78] In 1868 the Workers' Party was formed.[79] An organization of Negro workers was created.[80] As a result of the opposition of the workers, there were reductions in a number of states of bills prohibiting strikes.[81] However, the workers' movement in the USA developed under difficult conditions. The large fluctuation of labor impeded the formation of permanent cadres of the proletariat. The bourgeoisie succeeded in weakening the worker movement by bribing the workers' leaders, by creating employers' organizations, by urging worker-Americans against Negroes and immigrants, and by stirring up national differences among worker-immigrants from various countries.

[76] William H. Sylvis (1828–1869), president of the Iron-Moulders International Union, helped to organize the National Labor Union and became its president in 1868. Instrumental in agitating for the eight-hour day and other reforms, the National Labor Union collapsed by 1873 after having dissipated much of its trade-union activity in favor of political action and greenbackism.

[77] The Communist Club of New York propagandized for the abolition of "the bourgeois property system" and the implementation of "a sensible system under which participation in the material and spiritual pleasures of the earth would be accessible to everyone and corresponding, as much as possible, to his needs." The club subsequently affiliated with the Marxist International Working Men's Association. In 1872, the General Council of the International decided to move its headquarters from London to New York City, apparently in order to remove the organization from Bankuninist influence and infiltration. The International claimed an estimated thirty American sections with 5,000 members. In 1876, the American sections voted to dissolve in view of internal dissension, the formation of two rival Socialist organizations, and the dissolution of the International abroad.

[78] The Grangers, or the Patrons of Husbandry, organized for the general promotion of agricultural interests and fraternal purposes but soon expanded its activities into the political arena and prompted the organization of two powerful farm alliances: the National Farmers' Alliance, active in the Northwest, and the National Farmers' Alliance and Industrial Union, active in the South.

[79] Several labor parties, all of them politically inconsequential, were formed in the 1860's and 1870's, but there is no evidence of the organization of a Worker's Party in 1868. In that year, the German General Working Men's Union and Communist Club did merge to form the Social Party of New York and Vicinity.

[80] Organized in 1869, the National Colored Labor Union sought to organize Negro workers and co-operative associations. However, Negro Republican leaders captured control of the organization and subordinated its economic activities to partisan political action.

[81] No state statutes explicitly prohibited strikes, but laws did exist which made effective strike action impossible. By 1886, thirty-five states subjected labor activities to possible prosecution as criminal conspiracies and only three states legally encouraged the organization of trade unions and specifically exempted strikes from criminal conspiracy prosecution.

FROM RECONSTRUCTION TO THE FIRST WORLD WAR

annotated by O. LAWRENCE BURNETTE, JR.

The USA at the end of the 1870's to the 1890's: The development of pre-monopolistic Capitalism into imperialism.

IN THE PERIOD which followed the Civil War and the Reconstruction of the South, the USA changed into a highly developed industrial capitalistic country. In volume of industrial output it stood fourth in the world in 1860, but by 1894 it was already in first place. The abolition of slavery as a system, the vast expansion of the domestic market after the war, the availability of rich natural resources, the wide application of new techniques, the massive immigration to the USA from various countries, as well as the influx of capital from Europe contributed to this. The increasingly intensified process of concentrating capital was taking place. The activity of large-scale corporations and millionaires (Vanderbilt, Carnegie, Rockefeller, Morgan, and others) expanded. In 1870 the Standard Oil Company was formed, whose control by 1879 extended to more than 90 per cent of the oil industry of the USA. Other large monopolies were likewise formed in various branches of the national economy. In 1895 the National Association of Manufacturers (*q.v.*) was formed—the largest organization of USA monopolists. The activities of capitalistic monopolies (especially in railroad construction) were accompanied by the plundering of the government land reserve and the treasury, by monstrous speculation and corruption, which added particular acuteness to the economic crises. All the

forces of reaction united for the fight against the increasingly strong movement of the workers and farmers. A rapprochement took place between the Republican and the Democratic parties, which had turned into the parties of the upper bourgeoisie. The Republican Party was in power almost all the time (the adminstrations of A. Johnson, 1865–1869, U. Grant, 1869–1877, R. Hayes, 1877–1881, J. Garfield, 1881, Ch. Arthur, 1881–1885, W. Harrison, 1889–1893). The Democratic Party succeeded in winning in presidential elections only twice (the administrations of G. Cleveland in 1885–1889 and 1893–1897).

Customs tariffs were raised in the interests of the upper bourgeoisie, and a law was passed adopting the gold standard. The best land from the national reserve was turned over to speculators, railroad and other companies. A northern railroad company alone received about forty-four million acres of land.[1] The financial policy of the government, the high protective tariffs, the increase

---

[1] The reference is presumably to the Northern Pacific Railroad, chartered in 1864, which did receive a land grant totaling approximately 44,000,000 acres. While the total acreage grants to railroads in the West were large, and princely domains did fall into the hands of speculators through fraud and lax administration, the "best" land did not necessarily fall to either speculators or railroads; and the principle of land grants did expedite the national policy of encouraging the settlement of the West and establishing transcontinental communication. See J. B. Sanborn, *Congressional Grants of Land in Aid of Railways* (Madison, 1899).

in prices in industrial trade, and the plundering of the national land reserve by the upper bourgeoisie placed the farmers, who had fallen more and more into dependence on banks, in a difficult position. All this aggravated the dissatisfaction of the farmers and provoked an intensification of the farmer movement.

In the 1870's the farmers' Greenback Party (q.v.) was formed. In 1878 the Greenback Party united with workers' organizations and began to be called the National Workers' Greenback Party.[2] This party demanded the continued circulation of paper money (which in the mistaken thinking of the farmers would have to lead to the raising of prices on agricultural products), the restraining of capitalist corporations, the introduction of a progressive income tax, the lowering of protective tariffs, and the introduction of an eight-hour working day. In the congressional elections of 1878 the Greenback Party received over a million votes, but shortly thereafter the party collapsed for lack of consistent revolutionary leadership.[3] With the aim of weakening the farm movement Congress made several concessions to the farmers, having retained, notwithstanding the President's veto, the circulation of paper money. The economic crisis and the following depression (1873–1878) made the position of the working class acutely worse. In 1877 in the USA the unemployed numbered about three million.[4] Wages of workers declined 40 to 50 per cent. Strikes of the workers and rallies of the unemployed occurred all over the country. With the object of eliminating the power of the workers, legal reprisals were executed upon the workers' leaders. Thus, after a strike of the Pennsylvania miners (1874–1875) many of its leaders were sentenced to death or to long prison terms on fictitious charges. In 1877 troops suppressed a large-scale strike of railroad workers. In 1876 the Socialist Workers' Party[5] (SWP; in the beginning called the Workers' Party) was formed from several Socialist groups. F. A. Zorge[6] (q.v.), a German Marxist, student and comrade of K. Marx and F. Engels, living in the USA took an active part in the formation of the party. However, the SWP, weakened by sectarianism, did not become the party of the masses. The growth of the party and its influence with the masses was impeded by the social heterogeneity of its composition, by the construction of the party on the basis of individual national groups, and by its disregard of work in the trade unions.[7] In 1878 the Knights of Labor, (q.v.), founded before in 1869, became a lawful and masses' trade-union organization. In 1881 the American Federation of Labor was formed (AFL, q.v.), built on the guild pattern. The AFL—in which S. Gompers and other

---

[2] The greenback concepts of Edward Kellog received wide support among disgruntled farmers as a palliative for fiscal reaction and the expanding effects of the depression of 1873. The union in 1878 of the Greenback and Labor Reform parties was under the banner of the "National Party." Fred E. Haynes, *Third Party Movements Since the Civil War* (Iowa City, 1916), 92–93, 120–125.

[3] The decline of the Greenback movement after 1878 was more related to relief from the depression, a partial return of agricultural prosperity, and the resumption of specie payment, which made the free coinage of silver the more realistic and feasible goal. Haynes, *Third Party Movements*, 131–152.

[4] Unemployment resulting from the depression was aggravated in 1877 by the Great Railroad Strike of that year.

[5] Known more generally in American history as the Working Men's Party, a loose organization ideologically divided between Marxist and Lassallean principles. See Ira Kipnis, *The American Socialist Movement, 1897–1912* (New York, 1952), 7–10.

[6] Freidrich Albert Zorge (1828–1906), a "Forty-eighter," emigrated to the United States from Germany and became an early—although not generally regarded as influential—leader in the Socialist movement. An organizer of the American section of the First Internationale in 1872, he subsequently participated in the establishment of the Working Men's Party and attacked its leaders when they later diverged from the classic doctrines of Marx and Engels.

[7] The American Lassallean Socialists were largely dominated by German immigrants, who turned their energies to the formation of workers' political parties and to securing public support for producers' co-operatives, contrary to Marxist doctrine. See Kipnis, *Socialist Movement*, 8–10.

trade-union leaders who had pursued oppor-
tunist policies and were justly called the
"workers' lieutenants of the class of capitalists" seized the leadership—became a reform organization.

Further aggravation of the class struggle
arose especially in connection with the economic crisis of the 1880's. In several states
workers', farmer-workers', and farmers'
parties sprang up. The development of the
revolutionary, workers' movement manifested itself in a series of large-scale class
actions. In 1885 a widespread strike of
Pennsylvania miners took place; in 1886
a vast strike of the railroad workers. On
May 1, 1886, a wave of strikes and demonstrations rolled through the entire country.[8]
The demonstrators demanded the establishment of an eight-hour working day. In Chicago, where the strike was almost universal,
the demonstration of the workers under-
went attack by the police. During a meeting in Chicago on May 4 provocateurs,
aiming to enforce antiworker repressions,
threw a bomb which resulted in the deaths
of four workers and seven policemen. On
the basis of false testimony by provocateurs,

four organizers of the meeting were executed and many of its participants were sentenced to long prison terms.[9]

The struggle of the workers of the USA
for an eight-hour working day received the
support of the international workers' movement. At the first Congress of the Second
Internationale in Paris (1889), the first
of May was announced as the day of international solidarity of the proletariat and of
the struggle of workers throughout the
world for an eight-hour working day.

Aiming to strengthen repressions against
the popular mass movement, the large-scale
capitalists and landowners effected a series
of antidemocratic measures. A revision of
state constitutions, to strengthen local executive authority, began.[10] The National Guard
was reorganized; parts of it were subordinated to the federal General Staff. The
bourgeoisie stirred up racial and nationality
differences. Negro workers and immigrants
were subjected to cruel exploitation and discrimination. At the same time the American
bourgeoisie bribed the workers' aristocracy
and the trade union bureaucracy.

The American working class did not have
a militant revolutionary party. The Socialist Workers' Party, despite several positive
results of its activity, did not free itself from
the mistake of sectarianism and therefore
did not change into the party of the masses.
The leader of the party, D. De Leon,[11] ex-
posed the opportunists, but instead made his
own sectarian mistakes. The Socialist Workers' Party repudiated the work of the re-

[8] The movement for an eight-hour day was
widely supported by laborers all over the country,
but the Federation of Labor was impotent and the
Knights of Labor officially hostile, making all agitation esssentially local and unco-ordinated. The
movement was felt only in New York, Cincinnati,
Baltimore, Milwaukee, and especially, in Chicago.
Of an estimated total of 340,000 participants, 190,-
000 actually went on strike—80,000 of whom were
in Chicago. See Henry David, The History of the
Haymarket Riot (New York, 1936), 175–177.

[9] American historians are by no means certain
who threw the bomb in the Haymarket, or for
what purpose. Eight defendants, Chicago radicals,
were tried and convicted, in part on circumstan-
tial evidence, for engaging in conspiracy of incit-
ing a riot, of which the bombing was the intended
result. The propriety of the actions of the Chicago
police in quelling the riot has been questioned, but
there has been no conclusive imputation of sinis-
ter motives to the officials. See David, Haymarket
Riot, 253–285, et passim.

[10] The series of constitutional revisions at the
turn of the century in the states of the South has
been ably documented and interpreted by C. Vann
Woodward, in his Origins of the New South,
1877–1913 (Baton Rouge, 1951), 321–349, 369–

395, as a Bourbon repression of a rising tide of
democratic, racial, and economic unrest threatening to unseat the status quo. Additional regional
and state studies are needed to confirm the same
trend in other areas and to justify the extension
of the same interpretation.

[11] A native of Curaçao, after immigrating to the
United States Daniel De Leon became active in
the Socialist movement in New York. He first attracted attention through his strictures upon existing trade unionism, seeking to reorganize it on
a frankly Socialist basis. He regarded Gompers
and other Federation leaders as "labor fakirs" . . .
"doing picket duty for capitalism." In 1895 he
led out of the Knights of Labor a seceding faction, which was subsequently split by rebellion

formist trade unions. De Leon came forward in defense of the reactionary theory of "the uniqueness of American capitalism."[12] The sectarian mistakes of the SWP aided the reformists in carrying out a policy of dividing the Socialist movement. F. Engels sharply criticized the American Socialists, pointing out that for them Marxism was a dogma but not a guide for action.

The government pursued a policy of severe repressions against the workers' and farmers' organizations. In 1890 under the pressure of the antitrust movement the Sherman Act (q.v.), called "antitrust," was passed. However, this law was used for prosecution of trade unions and for the battle with strikes, actually helping the activities of the monopolistic combines. The number of monopolies increased sharply. Many farmers were ruined; 28 per cent of the total number of farms were mortgaged to banks. In 1892 a farmers' party, the Populists (q.v.), which many workers' organizations supported, arose. The party advanced a program directed against banks and capitalistic companies. In the presidential elections of 1892 the Populists received over one million votes. But in the elections of 1896 the Democratic Party took over the most popular Populist slogans in order to undermine their chances for further success. In 1895 a socialist professional and worker alliance was formed, the organizer of which was De Leon.

In the workers' movement the conflict of two tendencies—revolutionary and reformist—grew more acute. In the beginning of the 1890's miners were on strike repeatedly; in 1892 there was a powerful strike of metalworkers in Homestead (Pennsylvania); in 1894, a large-scale strike of railroad workers which had begun in the factories of the Pullman Palace Car Company (q.v.) in the suburbs of Chicago. The American Railway Union, led by E. Debs (q.v.), was at the head of the Pullman strike. The Homestead and Pullman strikes were suppressed by the government with the help of armed force.

The USA pursued an expansionist foreign policy. The American bourgeoisie strove to oust English capital from Latin America and to transform the Latin American countries into a source of raw materials and an exclusive market for the USA. With this object, the USA under the flag of Pan-Americanism (q.v.), summoned to a conference in Washington the representatives of the American States. As far back as 1867 the USA had succeeded in buying Alaska from the czarist government of Russia for the paltry sum of $7,200,000. Ruling circles of the USA pushed their expansion into Asia. In 1871 the USA undertook the policy of military invasion of Korea.[13] In 1882 it bound Korea to a one-sided agreement. In 1889 the USA signed an agreement with England and Germany concern-

---

against De Leon's "dictatorial" rule and ultimately became one of the founding elements of the Socialist Party of America. In 1905 he took part in organizing the IWW but soon lost his influence. W. J. Ghent, "Daniel De Leon," in *Dictionary of American Biography*, V, 222–224.

[12] Marxist doctrine rejected the contention that American capitalism was sufficiently "unique"— that is, sufficiently democratic—that it could be applied to the service of Communism.

[13] Devoted to naval promotion of American commercial and diplomatic interests in the Pacific, Commodore Robert W. Shufeldt, USN, in 1878 sailed to the Far East in the *USS Ticonderoga*. One of his objectives was the opening of the "hermit kingdom" of Korea, which had previously resisted any normal relationship with the Western world. Through the good offices of China, Shufeldt ultimately concluded a treaty on May 22, 1882, establishing normal diplomatic relations, the principle of extraterritoriality, the privilege of Americans to trade, and the liberty of residence in open ports, all of which were soon extended to other Western powers. There was no expressed or implied policy or threat of military invasion of Korea, and the treaty was concluded solely upon the basis of mutual advantage. The only protest raised by Korea was in answer to the United States Senate's imputation, during consideration of the treaty, that Korean sovereignty had been compromised by her recognition of a vague suzerainty of the Chinese Emperor. See Allan Westcott, "Robert Wilson Shufeldt," in *Dictionary of American Biography*, XVII, 139–140; and Charles Oscar Paullin, *Diplomatic Negotiations of American Naval Officers, 1778–1883* (Baltimore, 1912), 282–328.

ing a protectorate over the islands of Samoa. In 1893 the USA organized a revolution in the Hawaiian Islands and after that the Hawaiian Republic was formed with a government completely dependent on the USA.[14]

The USA in the period of imperialism (to the beginning of the First World War)

B Y THE END of the nineteenth century American capitalism had entered the stage of imperialism. The growth of capitalistic monopolies was taking place; the process of concentrating manufacture and capital had gained strength; the export of capital became more intensive; expansionist foreign policy swelled sharply. The entry of the USA into the imperialist stage was characterized by the growth of reaction in all policy, both in the spheres of domestic and foreign policy. The process of the concentration of capital in the USA took place more quickly and in a broader range than in other countries. After the crisis of 1900–1903, monopolies became the basis of the entire economic structure of the country. V. I. Lenin characterized American trusts as "the highest expression of the economics of imperialism or monopolistic capitalism" (*Works*, 4th ed., vol. 23, p. 32).

By the end of the nineteenth century the USA had outdistanced old capitalistic states in economic strength. Together with the growth of monopolies grew their supremacy over the economic and political life of the country and the subordination of govern-

ment authority to monopolistic capital. A financial oligarchy determined the domestic and foreign policy of the administrations of the Republican Party (the administrations of W. McKinley, 1897–1901, T. Roosevelt, 1901–1909, W. Taft, 1909–1913) and of the Democratic Party (the administration of W. Wilson, 1913–1921).

The administration of T. Roosevelt, trying to win favor among the popular masses, protested against the oppression of the monopolies, instigated suits against a number of trusts on the basis of the so-called "antitrust" Sherman Act. However, corporations escaped with small fines or revived under new names after their dissolution. The preservation of high custom tariffs (in 1909 customs tariffs on many goods were raised again) was favorable to the interests of monopolistic capital.

At the end of the nineteenth century in the USA, the worker movement gained strength. In 1898 E. Debs organized the Social Democratic Party[15] which formed the basic nucleus of the Socialist Party, formed in 1900–1901. The creation of the Socialist Party became a positive factor in the development of the workers' movement in the USA. However, this party did not become the revolutionary party of the working class. Reducing all political work to the struggle for position in Congress, it changed into a reformist party.

The government brutally suppressed the strike movement. In 1902 it frustrated by its intervention the strike of 150,000 coal miners who were fighting for a shorter working day, an increase of wages, and the recognition of trade unions. The leaders of the union of coal miners betrayed the interests of the workers and came to an agreement with the employers and the government. As in the domestic policy, the course of the USA in foreign policy was deter-

[14] The revolution of 1893 was organized by Americans in Hawaii, and its success was due largely to the support of the American Minister, John L. Stevens, and the interposition of American military force. The American intrusiveness was presumably without the prior knowledge or sanction of the government in Washington, as is here implied, and it was later disavowed by President Cleveland, who righteously undertook to restore the *status quo*. The provisional republican regime was kept at arm's length until annexation was consummated in 1898. For a recent treatment of the familiar story, see Sylvester K. Stevens, *American Expansion in Hawaii, 1842–1898* (Harrisburg, 1945), 187–299.

[15] The utopian Social Democracy of America was formed in 1897 by Eugene V. Debs and others. From it grew the opportunistic Social Democrat Party in 1901, under the leadership of Victor Berger. See Kipnis, *Socialist Movement*, 51ff.

mined by large-scale monopolies.[16] With the end of the nineteenth century, the striving to win a dominant position in the world market began to become more strongly apparent in the ruling circles of the USA. The USA declared its claims to a broad share in colonial expansion. However, by this time an agreement was already made among the other capitalistic states. The Spanish-American War of 1898 (q.v.), unleashed by the USA in April, 1898, was the first imperialist war for the redivision of the world. The USA compelled Spain, who had suffered defeat, to give up her transoceanic colonies. As a result of the Spanish-American War the USA seized the Philippines, Guam, and Puerto Rico and established virtual supremacy over Cuba, which from 1899 to 1902 was subject to American occupation. Under pressure of the imperialists of the USA the so-called Platt Amendment (q.v.), which gave the USA the "right" of intervention, was inserted into the Constitution of Cuba in 1901. Having taken advantage of the national-liberation movement in the Philippines in the struggle against Spain, the USA then brutally suppressed it (in 1899–1901). In 1898 the USA officially annexed the Hawaiian Islands. In 1899 an agreement was reached on the partition of the islands of Samoa between the USA and Germany. In 1903 the USA organized a revolution in Panama, as a result of which Panama seceded from Columbia. The USA established its virtual domination in the Panama Republic and in

1903 pressed a treaty on it,[17] in accordance with which it took the Panama Canal Zone (the construction of the canal was completed in 1914). In 1905–1907 the USA pressed an agreement on the Dominican Republic, according to which the American government took to itself the "settlement" of her foreign debt. The Dominican Republic was transformed into the object of the monopolistic authority of the USA. Trying to subordinate Latin American and other countries to its own supremacy, the USA made wide use of dollar diplomacy, combined with direct armed intervention and the suppression of liberation movements.

With the aim of furthering its expansion in China, the USA in 1899 proclaimed the so-called "open door" doctrine. Because of demagogic demands for "equal opportunities" for all powers in China, the aim of the USA to subordinate all of China to its own influence was hidden. The imperialist policy of the USA in China became apparent also in the suppression in 1900–1901 of the popular rebellion (1899–1901) in China against foreign oppressors.[18]

The administration of T. Roosevelt, having accomplished a broad program of foreign policy expansion, supported Japan in the preparation of a war against Russia. In the period of the Russo-Japanese war, 1904–1905, it gave economic, financial, and diplomatic assistance to Japan. The USA virtually gave Japan its consent to seize

---

[16] The role of corporate wealth in the origins and development of American imperialism has yet to be definitively established. The opportunities for overseas markets and sources for raw materials were dangled as bait before reluctant businessmen by expansionists and navalists long before economic realities secured business support for the imperial policy. Indeed, Julius W. Pratt, in his "American Business and the Spanish-American War," in the *Hispanic American Historical Review*, 14:163–201 (May, 1934), has shown that business leaders were opposed to the war if not to the principle of imperialism. See also Samuel Flagg Bemis, *A Diplomatic History of the United States* (New York, 1955), 463–475.

[17] The role and purposes of the United States and Philippe Bunau-Varilla in the Panama Revolution are well known. The Hay-Bunau-Varilla Treaty was hardly pressed upon an unwilling Panama as is here insisted. See W. D. McCain, *The United States and the Republic of Panama* (Durham, 1937), 16–18.

[18] The part played by the United States in the Boxer Rebellion consisted of stationing naval forces in Chinese waters and joining the international expedition in relief of the foreign settlement in Peking. While not insensitive to the opportunity of expanding American influence under cover of intervention, the United States resisted the temptations and were influential in curbing the designs on China by other intervening powers. For a recent discussion, see William R. Braisted, *The United States Navy in the Pacific, 1897–1909* (Austin, 1958), 75–153.

Korea (See Taft-Katsura Agreement). After signing the Portsmouth Peace Treaty in 1905, Japan closed the USA's access to Manchuria. Negotiations with Japan, having been accompanied by a demonstration of the strength of the USA Navy in the Far East, were concluded by the signing of an agreement between Japan and the USA in 1908 on the Pacific Ocean Basin (See Root-Takahira Agreement).

The revolution of 1905–1907 in Russia found a ready response in the USA. In a number of cities (Boston, San Francisco, and others), societies—"The Friends of Russian Freedom"—were formed. The impact of the revolution in Russia encouraged the strengthening of the workers' movement in the USA. In 1905 the trade-union organization "Industrial Workers of the World" (IWW) was founded, fighting for the organization of trade unions on an industrial basis (in contradistinction to the former guild trade unions). Large-scale strikes of miners took place (1907 and 1912); of longshoremen (1909–1910); of textile workers (1912); and of others. The IWW led many strikes; however, it tolerated serious sectarian mistakes; in 1908 anarcho-syndicalists seized the leadership through this organization. The struggle of the Negro people for their rights, a struggle against racial discrimination, assumed larger scope. In 1909 the National Association for the Advancement of Colored People appeared.

In 1912 a conference of the Socialist Party took place. The right-wing leaders of the party succeeded at the conference in passing a resolution in which the party in essence renounced the revolutionary struggle and declared the basis of its activities to be participation in the election campaigns. The worker's aristocracy—which the bourgeoisie bribed for the huge profits gained by it as a result of the increase in exploitation of the working class, of the farmers, and of the Negro people, and in foreign-policy expansion—furnished the social basis of opportunism.[19]

During the time of the presidential elections of 1912 a group headed by T. Roosevelt detached itself from the Republican Party, coming forward as the National Progressive Party (it disintegrated after the elections). In its election platform it promised to contend with the trusts, to introduce the most progressive factory legislation, and to carry out a number of other reforms. The program and propaganda of the "Progressives" was an attempt to save capitalism with the help of bourgeois reforms. As a result of the split in the Republican Party, the candidate of the Democratic Party, W. Wilson, was elected President, having received a small plurality of the votes. The candidate of the Socialist Party, E. Debs, received about one million votes. Striving to paralyze the growth of the socialist movement, Wilson declared that the "Era of the New Freedom" was beginning; however, his political course conformed completely to the interests of the large-scale monopolies.[20] The subordination of the government to the financial oligarchy increased. The Federal Reserve System of banks was established under the direct instructions of the monopolies. Reserve banks were supposed to consolidate the activity

[19] The historical Marxist view of the American labor movement is that it has been dominated by a self-aggrandizing aristocracy, treasonably selling out the larger interests of rank-and-file laborers.

[20] The statement that the Wilson Administration "conformed completely to the interests of large-scale monopolies" can not be justified by its pronouncements of its official conduct. The New Freedom originally represented a doctrinaire rejection of the Supreme Court's "Rule of Reason" in antitrust actions and of Theodore Roosevelt's toleration of bigness coupled with regulation of unfairness. The first draft of the Clayton Antitrust Act embraced this position in its attempt to strengthen the Sherman Act and to establish effective *legislative* prohibitions against restraint of trade. Wilson was later converted to the Progressive concept of *administrative* regulation within the general definition of unfair competition, which has probably proved itself to be more effective and flexible in curbing business excesses over the years. For the most recent interpretation, see Arthur S. Link, *Wilson: The New Freedom* (Princeton, 1956), 417–444.

of all local banks, and they received extensive rights in regard to issuing banknotes. A federal deliberative board,[21] into which the largest barons of financial capital entered, became the real leader of all financial policy. The Wilson administration resorted to repression for the suppression of strikes. The large-scale strike of miners in the state of Colorado in 1913–1914 was suppressed by troops.

[21] The Federal Reserve Board was established in 1913 under the Federal Reserve Act, the most significant piece of domestic legislation of Wilson's administration. The Act sought to establish a national fiscal reserve system, to diminish the concentration of fiscal power, and to institute an elastic currency—a compromise between the wishes of the bankers and the demands of the radical progressives. In a natural application of experience, bankers have been appointed to the Board, but their wishes have not always prevailed, and subsequent legislation has vastly extended the principles of governmental control of banking and a managed currency. See Link, *New Freedom*, 199–240.

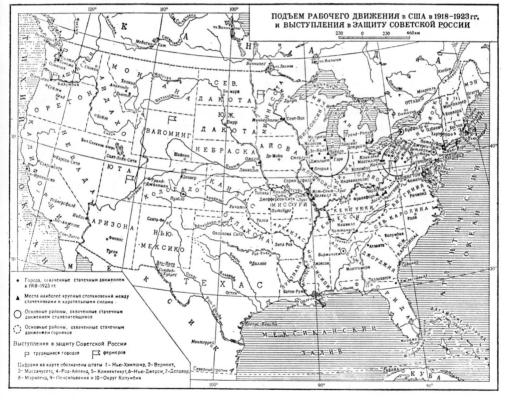

Map reproduced from the original text, showing centers of the workers' movement in the United States and places where speeches were made in defense of the Soviet Union, 1918–1923. In the accompanying legend, black dots indicate cities in which strikes occurred during this period; black triangles indicate sites of the greatest industrial strife; solid circles indicate the principal areas affected by steel strikes; broken circles indicate areas affected by strikes of miners; the flags, the first denoting industrial and the second agricultural localities, designate the cities in which pro-Soviet Union speeches were made.

FROM THE FIRST WORLD WAR
TO THE PRESENT

annotated by FRED HARVEY HARRINGTON

The USA during the First World War, 1914–1918

AFTER THE OUTBREAK of the First World War, 1914–1918, the USA declared on August 4, 1914, that it would preserve neutrality. American monopolies took to themselves the role of providing foodstuffs, ammunition, and loans to the belligerent states, mainly the countries of the Entente. An economic recession impending in 1913–1914 had already changed, by 1915 as a result of the war situation, into an upswing. American monopolists (especially the financial group of Morgan) made huge profits in deliveries to the European countries. The USA took advantage of its period of neutrality for military, economic, political, and ideological preparation for entry into the war. In 1916 a law was passed expanding the Navy, increasing appropriations for the Army and, in connection with these, increasing taxes. In August, 1916, the Committee of National Defense was formed, with the object of preparing for the mobilization of industry. The desire of the American monopolies to maintain maximum profits inevitably pushed the USA towards direct participation in the war for the redivision of the world.

Points of opposition existed between the USA and the countries of the Entente, especially England; however, in this period the conflict between the USA and Germany became particularly intense. At the end of 1915 Colonel E. House, Wilson's special confidential agent, announced: "The USA cannot allow the defeat of its allies, leaving Germany dominant over the world through a military factor."[1] Economic ties between the USA and the countries of the Entente strengthened substantially during the years of neutrality. American financial barons granted credit and loans worth millions to the countries of the Entente and feared to lose them in the event of a German victory. Tension grew still more in the relations between the USA and Germany in connection with the ruthless submarine war conducted by Germany.[2]

On April 6, 1917, the USA declared war on Germany. The period of USA participation in the war was characterized by the intensification in the country of political reaction, by the increase of militarists, by the transition to a military economy, and by a still more open submission of government authority to the monopolies. During the

[1] The House quotation should read: "It will not do for the United States to let the Allies go down and leave Germany the dominant military factor in the world." House to Assistant Secretary of State Polk, October 11, 1915. Charles Seymour, ed., *The Intimate Papers of Colonel House* (Boston and New York, 1926), II, 82.

[2] Economic forces had much to do with American entry into World War I. This account, however, overstates these factors (especially the financier influence) as compared with other forces. For a good treatment of the economic factors, see C. C. Tansill, *America Goes to War* (New York, 1938); for other interpretations, Charles Seymour, *American Diplomacy During the World War* (New York, 1934), Walter Millis, *The Road to War* (New York, 1935), and Ernest R. May, *The World War and American Isolation, 1914–1917* (Cambridge, 1959).

years of the war the living standard of workers declined.[3] Prices increased on foodstuffs and articles of broad consumption: in 1917 prices on foods increased on an average of 57 per cent, and in 1918 by 87 per cent in comparison with 1913; prices on clothes correspondingly rose 49 per cent in 1917 and 105 per cent in 1918. The increase of prices, the huge increase in taxes, the compulsory subscriptions to war loans, the growth of exploitation, the difficult wartime routine, and the presence—despite the economic boom—of a large army of unemployed led to a worsening of the condition of the working class. The workers responded to the increase of exploitation by numerous strikes. In 1917 over 4,400 strikes took place.

Wilson's administration dealt brutally with the worker movement. An espionage law (June, 1917) declared any anti-war rally of the workers to be treason against the government. Left-wing Socialists and members of the organization, "Industrial Workers of the World," courageously protesting against war, were subjected to repressions. Prominent figures of the American workers' movement, W. Haywood and E. Debs, were arrested. A split occurred in connection with the imperialist war in the Socialist Party of the USA, the internationalist wing of which, protesting against war, organized the League of Socialist Propaganda in 1915. The right-wing leadership of the Socialist Party openly supported an imperialist policy. The AFL pursued a policy of "class co-operation" with monopolies. A conference of the AFL in March, 1917, offered its assistance to the government in the event of entry into the war. The leader of the AFL, Gompers, was a member of a committee of the National Defense Committee.

Taking advantage of the fact that the strength of the European states was diverted by the war, the USA in these years increased its expansion in Latin America. In 1914, and again in 1916–1917, the Wilson Administration organized intervention in Mexico. The occupation of Nicaragua begun by the Taft Administration continued (lasting with a brief interruption until 1933). During 1915–1934 the USA occupied Haiti; from 1916 to 1924, the Dominican Republic. In 1917–1922 USA intervention in Cuba took place. In 1916 the USA forced Denmark to sell it the Danish West Indies.[4] During the time of the war the USA concluded an agreement with Japan at the expense of China (Lansing-Ishii Agreement, q.v.). However, this agreement was not able to check further intensification of American-Japanese differences. The war brought unprecedented profits to American monopolists. The average annual income of USA corporations in 1916–1918 was approximately $4,000,000,-000 more than the average annual income in 1912–1914.

The February bourgeois-democratic revolution of 1917 in Russia made American ruling circles, fearful of the withdrawal of Russia from the war, extremely uneasy. The USA hastened to recognize the bourgeois Provisional Government and supported it with huge loans.[5]

---

[3] Although the cost-of-living index rose as a result of wartime conditions, so did the index of real wages. See Paul Douglas, *Real Wages in the United States, 1890–1926* (Boston, 1930).

[4] Denmark was not forced to sell the Virgin Islands. Her voters and their Parliament were glad to accept the $25,000,000 offered by the United States. See C. C. Tansill, *The Purchase of the Danish West Indies* (Baltimore, 1932).

[5] The Wilson administration was far from satisfied with the Provisional Government, and never gave it all-out support. Recognition, however, was extended promptly—less than a fortnight after the overthrow of the Tsar. Further, the United States Government advanced nearly $200,000,000 in loans to the Russian Provisional Government between the spring and fall of 1917. In contrast, the United States extended no credits to the Bolshevik Government (which took over control in November, 1917) and postponed recognition for sixteen years. See William Appleman Williams, *American-Russian Relations, 1781–1947* (New York, 1952) and George F. Kennan, *Russia Leaves the War* (Princeton, 1956).

As a result of the First World War the USA was transformed from a debtor to the largest creditor, to whom the countries of Europe found themselves indebted for over ten billion dollars. Almost all the countries of the Entente fell into the debt of the USA. V. I. Lenin pointed out that American multimillionaires, more than anyone, profited by the war. The foreign trade of the USA grew substantially. Thus, in the period from 1913 to 1920 the trade of the USA with the countries of Latin America increased almost four times. Over half of the world's gold reserves was concentrated in the USA. The war stimulated further development of a number of branches of heavy industry. Several new areas of industry were developed. The process of centralizing capital grew. By the end of the First World War 1 per cent of the people controlled more than 50 per cent of all the wealth in the USA.[6]

The USA in the period between the two World Wars

A GENERAL crisis of capitalism began in the period of the First World War, and especially as a result of the defection of Soviet Russia from the capitalistic system. After the First World War the development of the revolutionary workers' and farmers' movement began in the USA. The impact of the Great October Socialist Revolution was of profound significance in strengthening the revolutionary movement in the USA.[7] In 1919 the number of strikes in the USA grew substantially. The most important were the strike of 365,000 steelworkers (of which the organizer was W. Foster) and the strike of 435,000 miners. In this same year powerful strikes occurred in the ports of New York and Seattle. Along with England and France, the USA became an accomplice in the intervention against Soviet Russia. The USA implemented open military intervention in the Soviet North and in the Soviet Far East (1918–1920).[8]

In January, 1918, Wilson came forward with an imperialist program of peace—the so-called "Fourteen-Point program."[9] Together with other imperialist states, USA tried to take advantage of the Paris Peace Conference of 1919–1920 to broaden the intervention in, and the organization of a blockade of Soviet Russia. Wilson achieved the inclusion in the Versailles Peace Treaty of 1919 (*q.v.*) of the Charter of the League of Nations. He strove to use the League of Nations in the interests of the foreign policy of the USA. However, the Versailles Treaty was not ratified by the USA Senate. A number of prominent bourgeois political figures (Senator Lodge, Secretary of State Lansing, and others) voted against involving the USA as a participant in the League of Nations,[10] in which England and France had leading roles. They protested sharply against the concessions to Japan effected by Wilson at the Paris Peace

[6] Although World War I did increase the concentration of economic control, the figures here presented are open to question. They are presumably drawn from Anna Rochester's heavily slanted *Rulers of America: A Study of Finance Capital* (New York, 1936), 144.
[7] Was there a strong revolutionary movement in the United States in 1919–1920, as this account suggests? This was the period of the Big Red Scare, when antilabor leaders and others insisted that the postwar strikes and unrest reflected a dangerous revolutionary trend. Historians, however, have found little evidence to support the theory that there was much danger of revolution.

[8] Some 5,000 Americans took part in an Allied landing at Archangel in northern Russia in 1918. One purpose of this expedition was to prevent supplies from falling into German hands. Nearly twice as many Americans were sent into eastern Siberia, to support anti-Bolshevik groups, to check Japan, and for other reasons. See, *e.g.*, Betty M. Unterberger, *America's Siberian Expedition, 1918–1920* (Durham, North Carolina, 1956) and George F. Kennan, *The Decision to Intervene* (Princeton, 1958).
[9] Some of the Fourteen Points were anti-imperialist, and this Wilson peace program—whatever its faults—stands in sharp contrast to the divide-the-spoils arrangements of the "secret treaties" of the Allies. For a general treatment, see Thomas A. Bailey, *Woodrow Wilson and The Lost Peace* (New York, 1944).
[10] Despite doubts about the League, Robert Lansing did not "vote against" it.

Conference and endangering USA positions in China. A majority of the Republicans (Lodge, Hoover, and others) opposed Wilson under the slogan of so-called isolationism.[11] Not having ratified the Wilson treaty, the USA in August, 1921, concluded a separate peace treaty with Germany, almost identical with Wilson's, but not containing the article on the League of Nations.

In conditions favorable for the growth of the masses' revolutionary movement, the Communist Party of the United States of America was founded in September, 1919, which carried on a struggle against the oppression of the capitalists and for the bettering of the position of the working class and of all workers. With the active participation of the Communists, large-scale strikes of dockworkers, who refused to load materials for the use of USA interventionist troops in Russia and for the White Guards, took place.

A campaign of protest against USA participation in anti-Soviet intervention unfolded across the entire country. American workers formed the "League of the Friends of Soviet Russia," which organized the gathering of signatures on a petition to the government to cease the intervention and blockade of Russia. Almost 100 trade unions joined in the petition. "Hands Off Russia" committees were also formed. In 1920 the American government was forced to recall its troops from Russia.[12]

In 1920 an economic crisis began in the USA, reaching its highest peak in 1921. In a number of branches of industry the volume of output declined 40 per cent or more. The number of unemployed reached 5,500,000. Wages were reduced. The crisis also gripped agriculture. Ruined farmers went to the cities, enlarging the ranks of the unemployed. The bourgeoisie intensified the attack on the rights of workers. Employers refused to negotiate with trade unions and broke off collective agreements. This policy was rebuffed by the working class. In 1921–1922 more than 2,500,000 workers participated in strikes. Over 600,000 miners took part in a strike of coal workers occurring in 1922. Railroad workers (about 500,000 men) were on strike simultaneously with the coal workers. The administration of the Republican President W. Harding (1921–1923), with the actual help of the AFL leadership, suppressed a number of strikes. The leaders of the AFL preached "class co-operation" with the capitalists, and helped them carry out the capitalist streamlining of manufacture leading to an increase in the exploitation of the working class.[13] The leadership of the AFL prevented the admittance into the AFL of Negroes and unskilled workers.

The struggle of the Negro people for democratic rights, and against the intensification of racial discrimination, was crushed by means of severe repressions. In 1917–1919 Negro massacres took place in a number of cities. In July, 1919, in Chicago, according to official figures, substantially underestimated, thirty-eight persons were

[11] Herbert Hoover, as well as a number of other prominent Republicans including William Howard Taft, favored the League.

[12] Pressure from American Communists and from non-Communist labor groups had little to do with the decision to end American intervention in northern Russia and Siberia. The collapse of Germany, Bolshevik successes, and general American reaction against overseas ventures, all figured in the picture, as did a growing realization of government officials and private citizens that the intervention had been ill-advised from the start. It is worth noting, however, that the Communist Party of the United States is first mentioned in this account in connection with efforts to assist Russian Communists. Theodore Draper's recent book, *The Roots of American Communism* (New York, 1957), argues convincingly that the American Communist Party was Russian-dominated from the start.

[13] This section shows Soviet attitudes toward American labor leadership, as other sections show Soviet attitudes toward American business. Much can be said against the AFL in the 1920's. The organization was ineffective in that decade, and declined in membership. It failed to make headway in the new mass-production, assembly-line industries. Many of its unions did exclude or otherwise discriminate against women, Negroes, and the unskilled. But for all of that, the AFL was not the antilabor force here pictured. For the question of AFL "cooperation" with capitalism, see Selig Perlman, *History of Trade Unionism in the United States* (New York, 1922).

killed and over 500 were injured, and hundreds of homes were demolished or burned.

After the war the economic and political role of the USA in the capitalist world grew considerably. The USA became the center of the financial exploitation of the world. American capital actively penetrated into the economy of many capitalist countries. Together with this, conflict sharpened, especially between the USA and England and between the USA and Japan. Harding's administration, in the interests of monopolies, maintained a policy of developing the expansion of the USA that became strikingly apparent in the course of the Washington Conference, 1921–1922 (q.v.). At the conference a five-power treaty was signed according to which the USA forced England to agree to the equality of the American and British battle fleets. The Anglo-Japanese alliance of 1902, which had strengthened the position of England and Japan against the USA in the Far East, was terminated. At the conference a treaty of ten powers was signed, on the initiative of the USA, which indicated the agreement of the imperialists concerning China. Taking advantage of its position as universal creditor, the USA, under the guise of maintaining an "Open Door" policy, actually strove for the maximum consolidation of its positions in China. Repeated proposals by the Soviet government for the normalization of relations between the USA and the USSR were rejected by ruling circles of the USA. In the period of partial, temporary stabilization of capital, which had begun in 1924, the chronic lack of employment remained; there existed underproduction in a number of branches of industry; the number of investors grew; and the export of capital increased (the export of capital in 1929 exceeded the prewar level more than four times). Capitalistic standardization led to the reinforcement of the exploitation of the workers and to an increase of the unemployed. The process of the ruination of farmers grew in strength.[14] In 1928 over 300,000 workers struck in the USA. Communists played an active role in leading the strikers.[15]

The defenders of American imperialism created a myth of so-called prosperity and of the "uniqueness" of American capitalism. They declared that American capitalism supposedly had its own proper development, completely different from the course of development of European capitalism, and that it did not fear economic crises. These "theories" about the "prosperity" and "uniqueness" of USA capitalism were propagandized in every possible way by reactionary trade-union leaders and other reformists trying to delude the broad masses of workers. In actuality the stabilization of capitalism which was characterized by the sharpening of conflict between the workers and capitalists, between the imperialists and the peoples of the colonial countries and among the imperialists of various countries, was as partial and temporary in the USA as in all the capitalist countries.

During the time of the presidential elections of 1924, a so-called Progressive bloc was formed representing the interests of the farmers and the petty urban bourgeoisie and supported by part of the trade unions. Its origin was provoked by the dissatisfaction of the workers with the policy both of the Republican and Democratic parties. The bloc advocated a program directed at the negligible democratization of government apparatus and toward the bettering of the situation of workers and farmers. Senator R. La Follette, who was advanced as the presidential candidate of this bloc, received a substantial number of votes in the elec-

[14] Although there was suffering in some quarters, the 1920's were a decade of prosperity for most Americans. For a general treatment, see George Soule, *Prosperity Decade, From War to Depression, 1917–1929* (New York, 1947).
[15] The Communists were unsuccessful in their efforts to secure control of the American labor movement in the 1920's. For a discussion of their efforts, see Daniel Bell, "The Background and Development of Marxian Socialism in the United States," in Donald Drew Egbert and Stow Persons, eds., *Socialism and American Life* (Princeton, 1952).

tions (after the elections the bloc collapsed).

The candidate of the Republican Party, C. Coolidge (*q.v.*), who was Vice-President during the administration of Harding and who had taken the presidential post in 1923 because of the sudden death of Harding, was elected President. The Coolidge Administration (1923–1929) continued proceedings against Sacco and Vanzetti[16] (*q.v.*), participants in the American workers' movement. Sacco and Vanzetti were executed on the basis of deliberately false charges (1927). The execution of Sacco and Vanzetti provoked a mass campaign of protest in the USA and throughout the world. The Coolidge Administration prevented the passage of bills to help ruined farmers. It raised protective tariffs in the interests of monopolies. The foreign policy of the Coolidge Administration was notable for its unfriendliness in regard to the USSR.

In 1923–1924 a reparations plan for Germany, the so-called Dawes Plan, was worked out (chiefly by American monopolists), having as its fundamental object the reviving of German militarism as a force directed against the Soviet government, and the creation of conditions for the establishment of the practical control of foreign capital, especially American, over the German economy.[17] In 1924–1929 the influx of foreign capital into Germany exceeded ten to fifteen billion marks in long-term investments alone; American capital investments constituted 70 per cent of the

total of all long-term loans. The USA, together with France, proposed the conclusion of an international pact on the "renunciation of war as an instrument of national policy" (Kellogg-Briand Pact of 1928). The USA and other imperialist powers strove to turn the pact into a means of isolating the USSR; however, under the pressure of public opinion they were forced to invite the USSR to subscribe to the pact.[18]

Aiming to maintain high profits for USA monopolies who were exploiting Latin American countries and to suppress the democratic forces of these countries, the Coolidge Administration continued military intervention in Haiti and likewise in Nicaragua where a liberation, anti-imperialist movement was spreading, and interfered in the internal affairs of Mexico and other Latin American republics. Striving to suppress the Chinese anti-imperialist and antifeudal revolution, the USA together with other imperialist powers carried out intervention in China.[19] USA warships participated in the bombardment of Nanking in March, 1927. The growing expansion of the USA led to the further aggravation of imperialist conflicts, especially Anglo-American and Japanese-American. In the 1920's Anglo-American oppositions became the principal conflicts within the capitalist world. A struggle for markets and for sources of raw

---

[16] The Coolidge Administration had no formal connection with the Sacco-Vanzetti affair. The case was handled in the Massachusetts state courts.

[17] The Dawes Plan was designed to strengthen the German economy and, indirectly, the economy of all Western Europe. American desire for European economic stability involved, among other things, concern over repayment of war debts owed by the Allies to the United States; interest in openings for American exports and capital; and desire to prevent developments likely to promote the growth of Communism. The Americans who worked on the Dawes Plan did not, however, desire to revive German militarism; nor did they contemplate building up Germany as a military bulwark against the Soviet Union.

[18] Soviet Russia was not invited to the signing ceremony. The United States and other Powers agreed, however, that the USSR should have an opportunity to adhere to the pact. Desire to secure a Russian pledge for peace, rather than public opinion, appears to have been the reason. See Robert H. Ferrell, *Peace in Their Time: The Origins of the Kellogg-Briand Pact* (New Haven, 1952).

[19] Some Americans called for Great Power intervention when the Chinese Nationalists acquired Russian advisers in the 1920's, and when anti-foreign sentiment led to riots, boycotts, and the like (fight "militarism, brigandage and Bolshevism"). The American Government, however, rejected such suggestions and generally pursued a "hands-off" policy. American-Chinese relations improved at the end of the 1920's, as the Nationalists gained strength and as Chiang Kai-shek drove the Communists out of the Nationalist ranks. See Dorothy Borg, *American Policy and the Chinese Revolution, 1925–1928* (New York, 1947).

materials, especially for oil, with the USA pressing England more and more, developed between the USA and England. In the middle of the twenties the export of capital from the USA was twice as large as the export of capital from England.

In the elections of 1928 the monopolist bourgeoisie sent to the office of President the candidate of the Republican Party, H. Hoover (President, 1929–1933). Hoover came into authority under the slogan of "prosperity." However, the destructive economic crisis of 1929–1933 graphically proved the failure of the "theories" of "prosperity" and the "uniqueness" of the course of the development of American capitalism. The world crisis most forcefully struck the principal capitalistic country— the USA, which by that time had concentrated in its hands approximately half of the production and consumption of the capitalist world. The economic crisis gripped industry, agriculture, trade, and the credit system; it was extremely severe and protracted. The crisis fell as a terrible burden on the shoulders of the workers. During the years of the crisis, wages of workers fell 60 per cent, and the income of farmers 59 per cent. In 1932 in the USA, according to official figures, there were 13,200,000 totally unemployed, an overwhelming majority of whom did not receive any kind of assistance from the government.

The crisis led to the sharpening of the class struggle. The development of the workers' movement began in the country; the movement of the unemployed masses spread, being under the direct leadership of the Communist Party.[20] The Communist Party organized demonstrations of the unemployed on March 6, 1930, in many cities, in which 1,250,000 persons took part. A "hunger march" of the unemployed was carried out in Washington in 1931 with demands for the introduction of unemployment insurance and the distribution of benefits. In 1932 there was a march of unemployed war veterans in Washington. Troops under the command of General D. MacArthur dealt brutally with the participants of this march. During 1929–1934 more than 3,500,000 workers participated in strikes. In 1932 and 1933, with the assistance of the Communist Party, national conventions of farmers took place which decided on the necessity of a united struggle—with the workers—against the yoke of the monopolies. The protest of the farmers against low purchase prices expressed itself in a refusal to sell farm products to monopolistic companies.

Hoover's administration, helping large-scale capital, placed the whole burden of the crisis on the shoulders of the workers. It established a financial corporation with a capital of $3,500,000,000, which was used for the subsidizing of monopolies with the object of saving them from collapse during the period of the crisis. At the same time the administration reinforced repressions against strikers. The so-called Scottsboro Affair (q.v.), having begun in 1931, the authorities of the State of Alabama tried to arrange the execution, on false charges, of nine Negro youths. However, intimidations and repressions were not able to impede the growth of the struggle of the Negro people against reaction. The organization of the Negro peoples' masses grew. In 1936 in Chicago there was a convention of the progressive National Negro Congress, which delegates from 551 Negro organizations, uniting 3,300,000 persons, attended.

During the period of office of Hoover's administration, USA expansion in the Latin American countries and in the Far East increased. After Japan began the usurpation of Manchuria in 1931, several American monopolies continued to furnish Japan with strategic materials and war supplies. Reviving the war-industry potential of Germany, whom the USA, England and France strove to set against the USSR, American monopolists took an active part in the drawing up in 1929 of the Young Plan.[21]

[20] Although the Communists tried to assume "direct leadership" in the United States during the depression, they were notably unsuccessful. This account greatly overstates their influence.

In the presidential elections of 1932, F. Roosevelt (*q.v.*), the candidate of the Democratic Party, won. F. Roosevelt was subsequently elected three more times (in 1936, 1940, 1944) and was President from 1933 to 1945.

After coming into office Roosevelt proclaimed the "New Deal," representing an attempt to overcome the crisis on the basis of "regulation" of private-capital activity, to strengthen the capitalistic system by strengthening government capitalism, and with the help of several concessions to the masses to keep them from revolutionary actions. Two acts, passed in 1933, underlay the "New Deal": The "National Industrial Recovery Act" (NIRA) and the "Agricultural Adjustment Act" (AAA). The NIRA established government regulation of industry, for which in various branches "fair practices codes" were introduced, fixing prices on products, fixing the level of production, regulating markets, establishing maximum working hours and minimum wages. The basic object of the codes consisted in mitigating the crisis by reducing production. A government administration, into which representatives of the large monopolies entered, was formed for the implementation of the NIRA. Having taken into their own hands the working-out of the "codes," the monopolists put into practice a policy of compulsory cartelizing, and reduced wages for workers. The profits of the monopolies increased sharply during the time of Roosevelt's presidency.

In practice, the National Labor Board established by Roosevelt guarded the interests of employers. The "Federal Emergency Relief Administration" attempted to solve the problem of unemployment by sending part of the unemployed to work camps for public works and by paying unemployment benefits. However, only a negligible part of the unemployed were occupied in public works, and only 20 per cent of the unemployed were given the small benefits.[22] At the same time, the government gave three billion dollars in aid to the banks.[23] A law regulating agriculture was supposed to raise prices on agricultural products. With this object the government distributed subsidies to the farmers for reducing the area under grain crops and for reducing livestock. The AAA was used with profit by the largest agricultural monopolies and market corporations, but, naturally, it could not prevent the mass ruin of the farmers.

In 1933 in the USA a slow rise in industrial production began, which, however, turned into its own depression. The attempt of Roosevelt's administration to overcome the depression and to prevent the approach of a new crisis with the help of the "New Deal" ended in failure.

In 1933–1935 the strike battle of the proletariat grew in strength. In 1933, 1,695 strikes took place; in 1934, 1,856 strikes; in 1935, 2,014 strikes. In the strikes about four million strikers in all participated. Strikes gripped the textile, steel, coal, automobile, and other branches of industry. In

---

[21] During the Hoover Administration, American influence declined rather than increased in Latin America. There was no real American "expansion" in the Far East at this time. When Japan invaded Manchuria, the American Government took an anti-Japanese stand (nonrecognition of conquests), not a pro-Japanese position as here implied. Like the Dawes Plan, the Young Plan was an effort to solve European economic problems, rather than an attempt to crush Soviet Russia.

[22] The emergency relief projects of the New Deal reached a larger number and had a larger effect than is here indicated. Although business men did help shape some of the first Roosevelt statutes (*e.g.*, NIRA), the New Deal had less of a Big Business flavor, and helped the bulk of the farmers and workers more than this account implies. See Basil Rauch, *History of the New Deal* (New York, 1944).

[23] The reference is presumably to a provision inserted by inflationary Congressmen in the Farm Relief and Inflation Act of 1933, whereby the President was given discretionary authority to inflate the currency by issuing $3,000,000,000 in new treasury notes ("greenbacks") or by reducing the gold content of the dollar by 50 per cent. Roosevelt did not issue the greenbacks. See Broadus Mitchell, *Depression Decade, From New Era to New Deal, 1929–1941* (New York, 1947), 137–138.

1934 a strike of textile workers took place. The general strike in San Francisco in 1934 had an extraordinary range, enveloping all of the Western seaboard. The Communist Party, constantly fighting for the united action of the working class and the farmers, was the organizer of many militant rallies. The Communist Party promoted an active struggle against the threat of fascism and war. The Ninth Congress of the Party (1936) called for the organization of a united democratic front of workers, farmers, petty bourgeoisie, and Negroes.

The Communist Party had substantial influence in left-wing trade unions, advocating the reorganization of the AFL on an industrial basis. In 1935 the Congress of Industrial Organizations (q.v.) was formed (the CIO, existing until 1938 under the name of the Committee for Industrial Organization).[24] In 1936 the reactionary leadership of the AFL expelled from the federation, trade unions (with one million members) which had joined the Committee for Industrial Organization. However, left-wing elements did not succeed in heading the CIO, whose leadership was seized by right-wing trade union leaders—Lewis, Murray, Carey, and others.

Under pressure of the workers, Roosevelt's administration made several concessions to the working class. In June, 1935, Congress passed the so-called Wagner Act (q.v.), in which the right of workers to conclude collective agreements with employers was declared. At the same time this act stipulated compulsory arbitration, with the object of breaking strikes.[25]

Under the conditions of a profound and lingering economic depression, the monopolies considered the majority of legislative enactments of the "New Deal" to be for

themselves. When a transition to an economic revival began to appear, the attitude of the monopolies toward "planned" experiments changed sharply and they demanded their cancellation. As a result, the Supreme Court in 1935 and 1936 held the NIRA and AAA to be unconstitutional, which meant their abolition.[26]

The foreign policy of the Roosevelt Administration in a number of questions was carried out by somewhat different methods from the policies of former administrations. On November 16, 1933, the USA established diplomatic relations with the USSR. By this the most far-seeing American statesmen recognized that the establishment of diplomatic relations with the USSR corresponded to the interests of the USA.

In connection with the growth of the resistance of the peoples of Latin America to the expansion of the USA, Roosevelt proclaimed in 1933 the so-called "Good Neighbor Policy," which in actuality, however, served as a disguise for the old policy of intervention in the domestic affairs of the Latin American countries. Reactionary circles in the USA promoted the organization in Mexico of the rebellion of General Cedillo against the lawful government of Cardenas (1938).[27]

In 1935 a neutrality act was passed in the USA giving the President the right to prohibit the export of arms to countries in

---

[24] The wording here suggests that the Communists had a great deal to do with the formation of the CIO. Such was not the case.

[25] The failure to mention such significant New Deal legislation as the establishment of Social Security, the Federal Deposit Insurance Corporation, the Securities and Exchange Commission, etc., should be noted.

[26] Most businessmen had ceased to support NIRA and were opposed to AAA in 1935 and 1936. There is no evidence, however, that the Supreme Court overthrew NIRA and AAA because of pressure from business. Rather, the decisions reflected the constitutional reasoning and social philosophies of the sitting judges.

[27] Under The Good Neighbor Policy as developed by Presidents Hoover and Roosevelt, the United States abandoned its "old policy" of military intervention in Latin America. By using diplomatic and economic rather than military methods, the United States was able to increase its influence in the area during the 1930's. Despite friction over Cardenas' expropriation measures, the Roosevelt Administration remained on friendly terms with Mexico in these years; and the United States Government assisted Cardenas during the Cedillo revolt. While some United States businessmen favored Cedillo, they failed to provide that general with effective support.

a state of war. Declaring the lawful Republican government of Spain to be "belligerent," the government of the USA deprived it of the right to buy arms in the USA. At the same time, the USA increased the export of strategic materials and arms to Italy and Germany, who were carrying out armed intervention in Spain (1936–1939). The USA did not consider Italy and Germany as "belligerents." In this way the USA took advantage of the Neutrality Act for the actual support of Italian-German intervention in Spain.[28] In March, 1938, the government prohibited the departure of American volunteers to Republican Spain, and in April, 1939, the USA officially recognized the government of Franco. Progressive forces in the USA actively protested against the Neutrality Act, demanding that help be given to the Spanish Republican government and that sanctions be used against Germany and Italy. Many American anti-Fascists went to Spain, where they fought in the international brigades.

In 1937 a new, world economic crisis began which again struck the USA the most severely of all the capitalist countries. Sixty per cent of the workers' families earned wages equal to only 50 per cent of subsistence wages, total unemployment benefits were reduced from $278,000,000 in 1936 to $96,000,000 in 1937, and public works were curtailed. In 1937 the number of strikes doubled in comparison with 1936 (4,740 strikes took place, in which 1,860,-000 persons participated). The Communist Party strove for the united action of the working masses of the USA, demanding that aid be rendered to the unemployed, and fighting against racial discrimination.[29]

In the 1930's the activities of a number of reactionary organizations in the USA became more energetic: the Ku Klux Klan, the American Legion (formed in 1919), and others.

In the prewar years the so-called isolationists played an important role in the conduct of the USA's foreign policy. Under the pretence of giving up intervention in the affairs of Europe, Asia, and Africa, the isolationists, representing in those years the most reactionary circles of the American bourgeoisie, in fact supported Fascist aggression.[30] The USA refused to support the proposals of the USSR directed toward the execution of a policy of collective security, toward a struggle for the preservation of peace, and against Fascist aggression. The USA facilitated the Munich Pact of England and France with Hitlerian Germany and Fascist Italy. Thus, the diplomatic representatives of the USA shortly before the conclusion of the Munich Pact (q.v.) carried on talks with the representatives of the ruling circles of Hitler's Germany, England, and France, from which it was obvious that the USA was not opposed to Hitler's aggression in the East. The USA's ambassador to Germany, H. Wilson, went to Prague in August, 1938, with the object of inducing the Czechoslovakian government to compromise with Hitler's Germany. The USA approved the negotiations of N. Chamberlain with Hitler in Berchtesgaden and Bad

---

[28] A Congressional resolution of January, 1937, barred exports to "either of the opposing forces in Spain." This helped Franco, although American policy makers did not intend that it should. See F. J. Taylor, *The United States and The Spanish Civil War* (New York, 1954).

[29] During this period Communist parties throughout the world tried to form "popular front" cooperation with non-Communist political groups. Such efforts were not successful in the United

States. The Socialists, Democrats, and organized labor all rejected united-front overtures; and the American Communist Party remained isolated and weak.

[30] Very few American isolationists "supported Fascist aggression." American opponents of the isolationists did maintain, however, that isolationist strength reduced President Roosevelt's ability to oppose Hitler and his allies. See William L. Langer and S. Everett Gleason, *The Challenge to Isolation, 1937–1940* (New York, 1952), an anti-isolationist view; for a contrasting interpretation, favorable to the isolationists, Charles Callan Tansill, *Back Door to War: The Roosevelt Foreign Policy, 1933–1941* (Chicago, 1952). See also Wayne S. Cole, *America First: The Battle Against Intervention 1940–1941* (Madison, Wisconsin, 1953).

Godesberg (September, 1938). The policy of the USA, like the policy of England and France, helped unleash the Second World War, 1939–1945.[31]

The USA during the period of the Second World War, 1939–1945

REMAINING formally a non-belligerent, the USA had already, with the very beginning of the war, come forward on the side of England and France. In November, 1939, Congress revised the Neutrality Act, allowing the sale of arms to the belligerents, which in practice meant authorization to export arms to England and France.

In the period of the Russo-Finnish War, 1939–1940, the government of the USA placed a "moral embargo" in 1939 on the export of goods to the Soviet Union, and gave the Finnish government a loan of ten million dollars. At the same time in the USA itself, persecution of the Communists and of all progressives increased. In 1940 Congress passed the Smith Act (q.v.), which subsequently was, in fact, used against progressive forces.

After the crushing defeat of France (June, 1940), the USA, preparing to enter the war, began carrying out a vast program of armament. In September, 1940, a law was passed for universal military service. The USA gave help to England in the fight against Germany. During the summer of 1940 it sold 1,000,000 rifles, 84,000 machine guns, and 2,500 pieces of ordnance to England. In March, 1941, the Lend-Lease Act was passed in the USA, allowing a substantial increase in the export of arms and war materials (mainly to England). But at the same time as it supported England against Germany, the USA tried to take advantage of England's difficulty to establish American control over several English possessions and spheres of influence. According to an agreement of 1940 (finally drawn up in the form of a contract, March 27, 1941) the USA received from England, in exchange for fifty old destroyers, ninety-nine-year leases on territory for the establishment of a system of American naval and air bases in a series of strategically important points on the Atlantic. Subsequently in the course of the war the USA concluded a number of other agreements with England, aimed at establishing her financial-economic dependence on the USA.[32]

In July, 1940, the USA achieved the recognition, at an inter-American conference, of the so-called Act of Havana, which permitted "any American country" to occupy any European possession in the Western Hemisphere, if it thought that this possession might be seized by one European power from another. In April, 1941, the USA established military control over Greenland, and in November, 1941, over Dutch Guiana.

On June 22, 1941, Hitler's Germany treacherously attacked the Soviet Union. Repelling the attack of the aggressor, the USSR entered the war. The Great Patriotic War of the Soviet Union, 1941–1945, began. The USSR took upon itself the main attack on Fascist Germany. The Soviet-German front became the decisive front of the Second World War. A powerful anti-Hitler coalition headed by the Soviet Union, the USA, and Great Britain was formed, which joined into a united camp, setting for itself the object of crushing Hitler's Germany. The formation of the anti-Hitler coalition answered to the interests of all freedom-loving peoples.

The conflicts between the USA and Germany by this time were extremely acute. The USA came into conflict with Germany

---

[31] The argument here is that World War II could have been avoided if Britain, France, and the United States had joined the Soviet Union in boldly resisting Hitler, instead of trying to appease the Nazi dictator. Views differ on this; but it does appear that the American public did not favor active involvement in Europe in 1938.

[32] American aid to Great Britain prior to our entry into the war was partially to offset the unfavorable balance created by the Hitler-Stalin nonaggression pact of 1939–1941, the existence of which is nowhere mentioned in the text above.

in the fight for the division of spheres of influence, colonies, and sources of raw materials. American capitalists were especially worried by the strengthening of the economic and political positions of Germany in Latin America. Together with this, the ruling circles of the USA and England could not leave out of account the desire of broad masses of their countries for close co-operation with the Soviet Union for a successful fight against Hitler's Germany.[33] On June 24 Roosevelt's government announced the support of the Soviet Union by the United States of America. On July 30 the personal representative of the President of the USA, H. Hopkins, arrived in Moscow, and on August 2 there was an exchange of notes between the USSR and the USA extending a working trade agreement for one year. On August 14 the Atlantic Charter was signed—a declaration of the governments of the USA and England regarding the war. From September 29 to October 1, 1941, there was a meeting of the representatives of the USSR, the USA, and England in Moscow, at which a decision was made on expanding the delivery of arms, equipment, and food supplies to the Soviet Union, and on the delivery by the Soviet Union of materials for England and the USA.

The military co-operation of the USSR, the USA, and England, which was established despite the differences in the economic and political systems of the countries entering into the anti-Hitler coalition, was extremely important in winning the victory over the bloc of fascist aggressors in the Second World War. The anti-Hitler coalition was a mighty union of freedom-loving peoples. The sympathy of wide masses of the American people increased more and more toward the Soviet people, who themselves carried the burden of the war with Hitler's Germany.

Side by side with the sharpening of the relations of the USA with Germany, the relations between the USA and Japan continued to grow worse. On December 7, 1941, Japan attacked the Pacific possessions and bases of the USA and England. American bases in the Pacific (Pearl Harbor) and in the Philippine Islands, on Guam and Wake Island, were subjected to attack. The American Navy suffered losses even in the first hours of the war. On December 8, 1941, the USA declared war on Japan. On December 11, 1941, Germany and Italy declared war on the USA. In June, 1942, the USA declared war on Bulgaria, Hungary, and Rumania. Thus the USA found itself in a state of war with Japan, and Germany and her associates (except Finland).

On June 11, 1942, a Soviet-American agreement was signed in Washington on the principle of mutual aid in conducting the war against the aggressor. In an Anglo-Soviet communique on a visit by V. M. Molotov, and a Soviet-American communique on the visit by V. M. Molotov to Washington, published June 12, 1942, in Moscow, London, and Washington, it was pointed out that at the negotiations "a full understanding was reached in regard to the urgent problems of the formation of a Second Front in Europe in the year 1942." Already by the summer of 1942 in England and Canada more than four million persons were in the army and in the USA more than two million; however, the Second Front was not opened either in 1942 nor in 1943.

Reactionary circles in the USA and England were not interested in the rapid conclusion of the war.[34] They wanted the mutual weakening of the USSR and Germany.

---

[33] There was little popular pressure in the United States for close co-operation with the Soviet Union, 1941–1945. Some Americans opposed co-operation. The majority agreed with President Roosevelt, who chose co-operation as a means of defeating Hitler.

[34] As this account suggests, Russian wartime relations with the United States and Britain were less cordial than were Anglo-American relations. The Western Allies wanted to win the war as quickly as possible; but, in order to hold their

In November, 1942, the USA and England carried out an invasion of North Africa, and in 1943, into Italy. In the Pacific Theater of war, the USA began active offensive operations against Japan in 1943.

During the period of the war the USA concentrated its armed forces in different regions of the globe important in regard to the economic, political, and military situation and important for the development of the sphere of influence of the USA. American bases were set up in Canada, Iceland, Greenland, and North Africa. The Second Front was not opened until 1944, when it became clear that the USSR was in a position to occupy Germany with its own forces and free Europe from the fascist yoke. In June, 1944, Anglo-American armed forces carried out a wide forced crossing of the English Channel and a massive landing of troops in North France, and, under the supreme command of the American Army General, D. Eisenhower, unleashed offensive operations against Hitler's troops. However, even after the opening of the Second Front, the main front of the war remained the Eastern Soviet-German Front, in which approximately 200 German divisions were concentrated (Germany kept only seventy-five divisions in the West). During the period of the war, several American monopolies encouraged ties with German monopolies, and a number of channels remained by which strategic materials found their way into Germany across Spain and Portugal.

During the time of the war the acuteness of the imperialistic conflict between the USA and England remained. The USA took advantage of England's difficulties for a widespread attack on England's positions; the USA was seeking to weaken the British colonial empire and to subordinate English colonial possessions to its own influence. In exchange for the delivery of arms from the USA, England found itself compelled to turn over to it part of its capital investments in the USA, in Latin American countries, and in Canada. In Canada the capital investments of the USA increased from $4,151,000,000 in 1939 to $5,157,000,000 in 1947, and English capital investments decreased in that same period from $2,476,000,000 to $1,668,000,000. Thus, even in the time after the war the political influence of the USA in Canada grew.

The USA took advantage of the war situation to push its expansion in Latin America. An overwhelming share of the export and import of the Latin American countries fell, in particular, into the hands of American monopolists. Having forced German and Japanese monopolies out of Latin America, the USA in the same way pushed out its English associates (England's specific share of the imports of the Latin American countries fell from 11.7 per cent in 1938 to 3.6 per cent in 1944).[35] A conference of the ministers of foreign affairs of the American countries, which took place in January, 1942, in Rio de Janeiro, created an inter-American committee for defense based in Washington, and sanctioned assisting the USA in building bases in Latin America.

During the period of the war with Hitler's Germany, the USA participated in a conference of the heads of state of the big

---

casualties to the minimum, they postponed invasion of France until their armed forces were fully equipped for the operation. The Russians, who were suffering heavy losses, became impatient at the delay, and refused to consider the Western Allies' invasion of North Africa and Italy as the establishment of a true Second Front. See Herbert Feis, *Churchill, Roosevelt, Stalin* (Princeton, 1957), and William Hardy McNeill, *America, Britain and Russia: Their Co-Operation and Conflict, 1941–1946* (London, 1953).

[35] England was unable to produce goods for export during the war years. This account stresses Anglo-American "imperialist" conflicts. Along with the conflicts, there has been, of course, much close co-operation. See footnote 34 above, and, for a survey, H. C. Allen, *Great Britain and the United States* (London, 1954).

three powers in Teheran (November 28 to December 1, 1943, *q.v.*) and in Yalta (February, 1945, *q.v.*). After the crushing of Hitler's Germany and the signing of the statement of unconditional surrender, the Berlin Conference of 1945 (*q.v.*) of the chiefs of state of the USSR, the USA, and Great Britain took place in Potsdam, near Berlin. In these conferences united decisions on the most important questions concerning the conduct of the war and the postwar organization of the world were reached by the three states. On July 26 the Potsdam Declaration of 1945, containing demands for the unconditional surrender of Japan, was signed by the chiefs of state of three powers—England, the USA, and China. But this demand was refused by the Japanese government. By this time the USA had achieved substantial successes in the war in the Pacific Ocean (the Pacific Ocean Campaign, 1939–1945, *q.v.*). In 1944 the USA had already taken possession of the Marshall and Marianas Islands; in 1945 American armed forces occupied the Philippines, seized by Japan in 1942, and took the Japanese island of Okinawa. Japanese military targets were subjected to heavy air bombardment. The USA achieved supremacy on the sea and in the air in the war with Japan.

In the beginning of August, 1945, American atom bombs were dropped on the cities of Hiroshima (August 6) and Nagasaki (August 9), which entailed the destruction of many thousands of noncombatant residents. The use of the atom bomb by the USA, in the opinion of many representatives of peaceable communities, was not called for by military necessity and had chiefly political objects.[36]

After the USSR entered the war with Japan on August 8, 1945, in accordance with having assumed this responsibility, and after the destruction of principal Japanese land forces by the Soviet Army, Japan surrendered[37] (the statement of unconditional surrender was signed September 2, 1945).

American capitalists, especially large monopolies, received huge profits during the war. At the beginning of the war the monopolies did not make arrangements to expand the production of war materials until they secured terms particularly profitable for themselves—large tax privileges and guarantees of high profits. In view of this, a substantial number of war enterprises were set up by the government at the expense of the federal budget. During the years of the war new businesses and new equipment, to the sum of $25,000,000,000, were put into operation. Of these the largest part was created directly at the expense of the government. The enterprises set up by the government were given over to exploitation by the large monopolies, and after the war they were sold to them at advantageous prices. The principal war orders (up to 70 per cent) came from the large monopolies. During the war the concentration of industry increased. In 1945 in the USA approximately the same amount of resources belonged to 250 of the largest corporations as had belonged to all the corporations in 1939. The profits of the monopolies increased sharply. In the period from 1939 to 1945 the total sum of the net profits of American capitalists reached approximately $60,000,000,000, as compared with $14,000,000,000 in the prewar period, 1931–1938.

From 1939 to 1944 the total volume of nonagricultural products doubled. The production capacity of industry increased approximately 40 per cent. The number of unemployed in 1944 was reduced by 700,-

---

[36] The main object of the use of the bomb was to secure total military victory with the fewest possible American casualties. See Henry L. Stimson and McGeorge Bundy, *On Active Service in Peace and War* (New York, 1948), 612–633.

[37] By early summer, 1945, key Japanese leaders recognized that defeat was inevitable. The American introduction of the atomic bomb and the Russian entrance into the Pacific War made further resistance seem altogether futile; hence the Japanese agreed to surrender on August 10. See Robert J. C. Butow, *Japan's Decision to Surrender* (Stanford, 1954).

000. The substantial growth in manufacture in the USA during the time of the war was possible, in part, thanks to the fact that the war activities were not carried on in the territory of the USA, and American cities did not undergo bombardment. However, the market created by the war situation could not insure a stable commodity market. Even in the period of the maximum development of war industry, production capacities were not kept running at full power. In 1943 industrial output reached its peak, after which its decline began. The gap between the productive capacity of industry and the purchasing power of American workers grew larger and larger.

In the war situation direct and indirect taxes were increased and inflation grew. All of this led to the reduction of the real wages of the workers. Employers violated collective agreements.[38]

The American people made an important contribution in the matter of the struggle of freedom-loving peoples against fascistic aggression. Striving to help in the victory over the enemy, the workers of the USA by their strenuous labor contributed to the increase in production of war products. In the years of the war the organization of the working class of the USA grew. The number of members of trade unions in 1941 was about ten million, in 1944, over fourteen million.

The Communist Party in the USA urged the workers to spare no efforts to achieve a victory over fascistic states. The Communist Party demanded from the government of the USA the fulfillment of its obligations in opening the Second Front.

During the years of the Second World War the Communist Party carried on a struggle with Browderism. E. Browder, who had elbowed his way into the leadership of the Communist Party, together with his henchmen attempted in 1944 to abolish the Communist Party under the guise of "reorganizing" it into a Communist Political Association. The main part of the Communists, headed by W. Foster and E. Dennis, remained faithful to the cause of the working class and succeeded in July, 1945, in calling a special convention in which a decision was made on the restoration of the Communist Party. Browder was expelled from the Party.[39]

In November, 1944, the regular presidential elections were held. F. Roosevelt was again elected President, for the fourth time. The broad masses of voters cast their ballots for Roosevelt in large measure because he declared the necessity of carrying on the struggle for the quickest possible victory over fascist aggressors.

The USA after the Second World War

AS A RESULT of the Second World War, Germany and Japan were put out of action as competitors of the USA. The USA was the only capitalist country to come out of the war with strengthened economic and military positions. However, after the end of the war, the USA ran into great difficulties. In connection with the stopping of war orders there was a decline in industrial production. In 1945, in the USA as a whole, industrial production was reduced by approximately 15 per cent; the output of the manufacturing industry by 17 per cent in comparison with 1943; and construction by more than 66 per cent in comparison with 1942. In connection with the sharp reduction of deliveries under Lend-Lease, exports fell to $9,800,000,000 in 1945 as compared with $14,400,000,000 in 1944. Unemployment increased. Speculation increased and inflation grew.

In 1945–1946 large-scale strikes occurred, particularly of steelworkers and work-

---

[38] While emphasizing wartime and postwar economic difficulties, this account fails to mention the striking rise in living standards in the United States since the 1930's.

[39] For a detailed account, stressing Moscow domination of the American Communist Party, see David A. Shannon, *A History of the Communist Party of the United States Since 1945* (New York, 1959).

ers in the automobile industry. The co-operation of white and Negro workers grew closer. In the postwar years nearly 1,500,-000 Negro workers were organized into trade unions.

With the purpose of maintaining the huge wartime profits, American monopolies tried to insure a high standard of production, which in its turn rested on the problems of a fight for new foreign markets, for supremacy in the world market for raw materials, and of the increase in export goods and capital.

In order to maintain high profits in the situation of a decline in the purchasing power of the people, American monopolies began to speed up the export of commodities in every possible way, making maximum use for this of the postwar situation in war-ravaged countries. With the help of a number of measures, American capitalists achieved some increase in the production level. However, by the end of 1948 exports had already declined (from $15,400,000,-000 in 1947 to $12,700,000,000 in 1948); a decline in industrial production began. With the end of 1948 an economic crisis began to develop in the USA, which was checked by the increasingly intense armaments race in connection with the Korean War. Imperialist circles in the USA looked for a way out of the mounting difficulties by further development of foreign policy expansion, which involved a reversion to production of war metals, an armaments race, a return to the system of military deliveries, and vast government appropriations for war manufactures. In the period 1946–1953 the total sum of military expenditures by the USA, including expenditures for arms for member-countries of the North Atlantic bloc, were almost $250,000,-000,000. After the Second World War the role of the National Association of Manufacturers in the political life of the country expanded even more. Monopolies, subordinating government apparatus to themselves even more, had a definite influence in both the domestic and foreign policy of the USA.

On April 12, 1945, the President of the USA, F. Roosevelt, died and the Vice-President, H. Truman, took the office of President. The influence of reactionary circles gained strength in the government of the USA. After the end of the Second World War the USA abandoned the concerted policy followed by the participants in the anti-Hitler coalition during the years of the war, rejected co-operation with the USSR and launched the "Cold War" against it.

In the postwar period the USA openly advanced its pretensions to "world leadership." Its course, aimed at the establishment of world supremacy of American monopolies and at the preparation of a war against the countries of the Socialist camp, was known as a policy "from a position of strength."[40]

The USA secured a large number of military bases on the territory of other states—in England, France, West Germany, and a number of other European countries, in many Latin American countries, in Asia, Oceania, and Africa. Immediately after the end of the war, the USA began to pursue a policy of remilitarizing the western part of Germany. In China, the faction of Chiang Kai-shek, supported by American aid, unleashed a civil war in an attempt to crush the democratic forces of the country. The USA set up bases in China and kept its troops on Chinese territory. Fortifying their position in China, American imperialist circles concealed the conclusion of various kinds of inequitable treaties and agreements with the Chinese government, as for example, a Chinese-American "friendship, trade and navigation agreement" (1946), and a Chinese-American agreement for economic aid (1947). The total amount of loans and the cost of other kinds of material aid given to Chiang Kai-shek's govern-

[40] This account pictures American foreign policy after 1945 in terms of imperialist expansion and hostility to the Soviet bloc. Other students see Communist expansion forcing American action, or the conflict of two expanding forces.

ment by the USA reached six billion dollars in 1949.

In March, 1947, in President Truman's message to Congress the so-called Truman Doctrine (q.v.), expansionist in essence, was formulated. Systematically intervening in the affairs of Latin American countries, reactionary circles in the USA encouraged the organization of revolutions in a number of Latin American countries (in Bolivia in 1946, in Venezuela in 1948, and others). In October, 1950, the USA obtained approval of the Inter-American Agreement for Mutual Aid (put into effect in 1948). The USA supported the Netherlands' war against the people of Indonesia, 1945–1948. In 1947 the USA concluded a military agreement with Iran, establishing the virtual control of American advisers over the Iranian Army. The USA gave help to France while it carried on a war against the peoples of Indo-China.[41]

In the USA itself, repressions against the workers' movement and progressive organizations were gaining in strength.[42] In 1947 the Congress of the USA passed the anti-worker Taft-Hartley Act (q.v.), directed against strikes and depriving the trade unions of many rights. In the same year Tru-

man's order for "proof of loyalty" of government workers was put into effect. On the basis of this order the dismissal of democratic elements from governmental staffs began. Various committees of the American Congress also widely expanded their activities of investigation, especially the "Committee for the Investigation of Un-American Activities." This committee instigated the prosecution of a great number of progressive journalists, motion picture figures (the investigation of "subversive" activities in Hollywood, which had begun in 1947), and trade-union workers. Numerous reactionary organizations—the Ku Klux Klan, the American Legion, and others—put new life into their activities.

In 1948 the presidential elections took place. Truman, the candidate of the Democratic Party, was elected President. The Truman Administration rested on a so-called two-party bloc of the Democratic and Republican parties. The Progressive Party, created in 1948, which united mainly the representatives of the progressive intelligentsia and several strata of the bourgeoisie and farmers, entered the elections side by side with the two parties of monopolistic capital—the Democratic and Republican parties. The Party advanced a program of a fight for peace and for the democratic rights of the American people.

In 1949 legal proceedings were instituted against eleven leaders of the Communist Party of the USA, who were sentenced to long-term imprisonments. Following that, a series of new legal processes were organized against figures of the USA Communist Party. Investigations of all progressive figures grew more intense. Reformist trade-union leaders supported the policy of militarizing the country and of attacking progressive forces. The leaders of the Congress of Industrial Organizations (CIO) introduced, at the convention of the CIO in 1949, a resolution approving the entire policy of the ruling circles of the USA. In 1949-1950 a number of progressive trade unions, with nearly one million members,

---

[41] Here and elsewhere in this essay, American foreign policy since World War II is presented as pro-colonial and as hostile to the aspirations of the common people of Asia, Africa, and Latin America. Any student of the period will admit that the United States has made mistakes and has suffered setbacks in these areas. It is also clear, however, that Americans have given valuable assistance to Asians, Africans, and Latin Americans in the years since 1945, and have often acted in the interests of those people as well as the people of the United States.

[42] As we all know, international misunderstandings often center around differences in the meaning of words. We note that this article uses "progressive" (along with "democratic," "worker," "supporter of peace," and "Socialist") to mean Communist or pro-Soviet; also, sometimes but not always, the terms embrace non-Communist Socialists, liberals and reformers, and conservative and liberal champions of civil liberties. At other points, however, the latter groups are lumped generally with the Democrats, Republicans, business and labor leaders, and intellectuals as "reactionary," "monopolist," and "imperialist."

were expelled from the CIO. In 1949 the CIO left the World Federation of Trade Unions.

Using the "Marshall Plan" adopted in 1948, the USA consolidated its control over the economies and politics of a number of Western European countries. The USA, together with England and France, pursued a policy directed at deepening the division of Germany. In 1949 the aggressive, military North Atlantic bloc was formed.

In June of 1950 the USA intervened in the civil war in Korea and after that introduced into the United Nations a resolution for the participation of states—members of the UN—in the Korean War. However, the governments of several capitalistic countries, having committed themselves to help the USA in Korea, were forced by the pressure of public opinion to limit themselves to basically negligible participation in the Korean War.[43] American armed forces, principally, carried on the Korean War. Reactionary circles in the USA did not wish to reconcile themselves to the failure of their plans in China which had followed as a result of the victory of the Chinese peoples' revolution (1949) and the crushing of the troops of Chiang Kai-shek. In June, 1950, the American Navy encroached upon Chinese territorial waters off the island of Taiwan, and following this, American armed forces virtually occupied Taiwan.

In December, 1950, Truman's administration declared a "state of emergency" in connection with the Korean War. The number of American armed forces substantially increasing, American monopolies took advantage of the war in Korea to make huge new profits. The profits of capitalists grew from $27,100,000,000 in 1949 to $42,900,-000,000 in 1951. American monopolies again began to get tax privileges for the development of war industry. Side by side with this, even within a year and a half after the start of the Korean War, taxes on individuals increased more than $16,000,-000,000.

A temporary increase in industrial production was observed in connection with the Korean War. Wide-scale deliveries of American arms to other countries, on the basis of the so-called "Mutual Security Guarantee" Act passed by the USA Congress in 1951, also contributed to this. Likewise, in accordance with this act $100,-000,000 was appropriated to finance undermining activities against the countries of the democratic camp.

The military draft (nearly one million men in 1951 alone) and the development of war production could not prevent the growth of unemployment, which had appeared as a result of the reduction of branches of civilian production. In 1952, despite the increase in war production, there were no less than three million totally unemployed. Besides this, there was a great number of partially unemployed. In 1953 the net income of the farmers of the USA, in comparison with the average income of 1946–1948, declined 35 per cent.

In the postwar period in the USA, a number of antidemocratic laws were passed. In addition to the antiworker Taft-Hartley Act passed in 1947, the McCarran-Wood Act, directed against the Communist Party and all democratic organizations, was passed in 1950. This act provided for the use of a number of restrictive and repressive measures against the Communist Party and also against persons suspected of contact with Communists or of sympathy for them. The McCarran-Walter immigration and naturalization act, directed against progressives—in the first instance against progressive elements among immigrants—was passed in 1952.

The policy of segregation and racial discrimination against Negroes continued; a number of legal actions against Negroes were organized. Thus, in 1949 in Martinsville, occurred the trials of seven Negroes, who were falsely accused of the rape of a

---

[43] Few other powers planned to participate in the Korean War on a large scale.

white woman and who were sentenced to death and executed in February, 1951.[44]

Progressive forces, and most of all the working class of the USA, came forward in defense of their rights. In 1950 there were 4,843 strikes with a total participation of 2,810,000 persons; in 1951 there were 4,737 strikes in which 2,220,000 persons participated; in 1952 there were 5,117 strikes with 3,540,000 persons striking. In March, 1949, in New York there was a convention of cultural workers in defense of peace. By November 1, 1950, two million Americans had signed the Stockholm Appeal to ban atomic weapons. During the period of the war in Korea a movement sprang up under the slogan, "Hands Off Korea!" New organizations of supporters of peace began to spring up: the Information Center of the Supporters of Peace (formed in 1950); the "National Committee of the American Trade Union Convention in Defense of Peace;" the organization of the "March of Americans for Peace;" and others. A number of farmers' organizations came forward in defense of peace (the conventions of farmers of Iowa in 1951, Pennsylvania, New Jersey, and others). During the summer of 1951 there was a Peoples' Congress in defense of peace, in which 5,000 delegates participated. The convention elected a National Committee to lead the peace movement.[45] The Negro people took an active part in the struggle for peace. The group of American Quakers came forward in support of peace. However, the peace movement in the USA was weaker than in many other countries.

As early as 1951 the USA by a one-sided act broke off the existence of trade relations between the USA and USSR. Following that, the Congress of the USA passed a law (the so-called Battle Act) whose aim was to compel countries receiving American aid to discontinue trade with the USSR, the Chinese Peoples' Republic, and the European countries of peoples' democracies.

In September, 1951, simultaneously with the signing of the San Francisco separate peace treaty with Japan (q.v.), the USA concluded a military treaty with Japan (a so-called "security pact"), according to which the USA received the right to keep its armed forces in and around Japan for an indefinite time.

Even in August, 1951, the USA had signed a pact for "mutual defense" with the Philippines. In September, 1953, the USA concluded an agreement with Spain for the establishment of American military bases on Spanish territory. In March, 1954, an American-Japanese agreement for "help in safeguarding mutual defense" was concluded. The penetration of American monopolies into the colonies and "spheres of influence" of Western European countries grew deeper. For the penetration into colonial and dependent countries, American monopolies made wide use of agreements signed in accordance with the so-called Point Four Truman program declared in 1949. In the post-war period the intervention of the USA into the affairs of Latin American countries increased. In 1952 reactionary circles in the USA encouraged the organization of a military coup d'état in Cuba.

The expansionist policy of the USA led to the aggravation of opposition among imperialist countries, the chief of which was the conflict between the USA and England. The struggle sharpened between the USA and England for control of English colonies and dominions. The USA has military bases in Canadian territory and keeps soldiers there. In September, 1951, the USA concluded a "mutual defense" pact with Australia and New Zealand (without participation by England). American capital took even deeper root in French, Belgian, and Portuguese colonial possessions. During the postwar years the penetration of

[44] Here as in earlier sections, this account details the sufferings without mentioning the general improvement in the lot of American Negroes.

[45] The term "peace movement" is used here in a special sense—mainly with reference to opposition to American policy in Korea.

American monopolies into the countries of Southeast Asia increased.

The USA waged an attack on the still-remaining English positions in Latin America. With the aid of an international petroleum consortium formed in 1954, American monopolies took control of a large part of Iranian oil which formerly belonged to English capital. Conflicts of the USA with other capitalistic countries sharpened still more in connection with the increasing competition of West Germany and Japan (in Latin America and other areas).[46]

In the presidential elections which took place in 1952, the Progressive Party advanced B. Hallinan as its candidate for President. The Communist Party and other progressive organizations of the USA came forward in support of him. A. Stevenson was the candidate of the Democratic Party and General D. Eisenhower, whom a majority of the largest USA monopolies supported, was the candidate of the Republican Party. Eisenhower, who had promised during his pre-election campaign to halt the Korean War, was elected President. Representatives of the largest monopolies occupied the most important posts in the administration. The 83rd Congress of the USA passed a number of laws in 1953–1954 transferring to the monopolies a substantial number of enterprises set up at the expense of the government budget. According to a coastal tidelands law, signed in 1953, the offshore oil deposits of four seacoast states were turned over to these states, which in effect meant the transfer of these oil deposits to large-scale oil companies. Taxes on excess profits were removed.

In Korea, American troops suffered setbacks. The Korean Peoples' Army and the Chinese Peoples' Volunteers halted the attack of the troops of the USA and other countries who were participating in the Korean War, and inflicted a large loss on

them. World public opinion demanded the cessation of the war in Korea.

In July, 1953, the USA began to conclude a truce in Korea. However, in October, 1953, the USA signed a so-called "mutual defense" pact with South Korea providing for the maintenance of American armed forces in South Korean territory. Despite the cessation of war activities, the state of emergency in the USA instituted by Truman's administration was not rescinded.

In February, 1953, thirteen prominent figures in the Communist Party were sentenced to various terms of imprisonment. In August, 1954, the so-called 1954 Act for control over Communist activities, passed by Congress and known also as the Humphrey-Butler or the Brownell-Butler Act, was signed by the President. This law was aimed at the virtual prohibition of Communist Party activities and against trade unions as well. The Progressive Party and many other progressive organizations (over 250 in all) were included in the list of "subversives."

Instances of violence against Negroes took place. A protest movement spread in connection with the murder of a Negro boy, E. Till, by racists in the state of Mississippi and the subsequent acquittal of his murderers, as well as in connection with other acts of violence in the country by racists. The National Association for the Advancement of Colored People, which was widely supported by trade unions, placed this protest movement in the forefront. Many trade unions organized meetings in which a demand was made for the stopping of racial discrimination and repressions against Negroes.

The Republican Party suffered a defeat in the Congressional elections which occurred in November, 1954. As a result of the elections, the Democratic Party won a majority (although a small one) of seats.

In the middle of 1953 a decline in production began, continuing until the fall of 1954. The index of industrial production

[46] Although there was competition and conflict among the Western nations, the Korean War period also brought increased co-operation within the Western bloc.

from July of 1953 to March–April of 1954 fell 10 per cent. By the end of 1954, even according to official figures, the number of totally unemployed was 3,230,000 persons. At the end of 1954 some rise in production began, products for war uses constituting 25 per cent of the total gross output of American industry.

The strike movement after the Second World War is characterized by the following figures: 43,700 strikes occurred in all in the period from 1946 to 1954, with a participation of 27,300,000 persons, as compared with 20,000 strikes involving 9,000,000 participants in the period from 1930 to 1939. In 1953, according to more precise figures, 5,091 strikes took place with participants numbering 2,400,000 persons. According to incomplete official figures, in 1954 there were 3,468 strikes, in which 1,530,000 persons took part. At the time of the strike of electricians and radio technicians in Detroit in 1954, police used clubs and tear gas. In 1955 strikes occurred in the automobile, steel, mining, and other branches of industry. Workers of General Motors Corporation, the Chrysler Corporation, the Ford Motor Company, United States Steel Corporation, and others were on strike. In 1955, according to preliminary figures, 4,200 strikes took place in all, in which 2,750,000 persons participated. In 1955 in the USA there were, according to official figures, nearly 3,000,000 totally unemployed and more than 9,000,000 partially unemployed.[47]

At the convention taking place in December, 1955, a united trade-union organization was formed, combining the AFL and CIO and taking the name of the American Federation of Labor—Congress of Industrial Organizations. The leadership of this organization remained in the hands of the right-wing trade-union leaders.

[47] The heavy emphasis on strike and unemployment statistics tends to obscure the fact that employment levels and living standards were very high in the United States during this period.

In January and February of 1954, in Berlin there was a Four-Power Conference of Foreign Ministers (q.v.), called together on the initiative of the Soviet Union. The USA declined the USSR proposal for the solution of the German question in a democratic spirit, and protested against the proposal of the USSR for the creation of a European system of collective security. Together with this, an agreement was reached at the Berlin Conference for a meeting of the Foreign Ministers at Geneva with the Foreign Ministers of all the five powers participating— the USSR, the USA, France, Great Britain, and the Chinese Peoples' Republic. At the Geneva Conference of Foreign Ministers (q.v.), the problem of restoring peace in Indo-China was successfully resolved. However, because of the positions of some delegations, especially the USA delegation, no agreement was reached on a final peace settlement in Korea. The Geneva Conference did play a favorable role in promoting the easing of international tension.

However, soon after the end of the Geneva Conference in 1954, a Manila Conference was called in September, 1954, at the initiative of the USA, as well as of England and France. At this conference the "South East Asia Treaty Organization" was signed, the so-called SEATO, setting up the formation of an aggressive military bloc in the area of Southeast Asia. In December, 1954, the USA concluded a "mutual security" pact with the Chiang Kai-shek faction, and in accordance with its conditions virtual occupation of the Chinese islands of Taiwan and the Pescadores by the United States is extended for an indefinite period. In January, 1955, the Congress of the USA gave the President the right, in the case of armed conflict in the Strait of Taiwan zone, to use USA armed forces against the Chinese Peoples' Republic.

Reactionary circles in the USA, with the aid of hired soldiers, organized armed intervention in June of 1954 in Guatemala, whose government was beginning to put into practice an agrarian reform and had begun to follow an independent policy. As a result of the intervention, the rightful government of Guatemala was overthrown. The expansion of USA monopolies met the growing resistance of the popular masses as well as of the dissatisfied circles of the national bourgeoisie of Latin American countries. In Latin American countries, especially, the struggle for the nationalization of natural resources being plundered by North American monopolies, grew stronger. At the Caracas Pan-American Conference, which took place in 1954, resolutions were passed despite the opposition of the USA for agrarian and other reforms especially directed against the economic expansion of the USA in Latin America.

In October, 1954, the USA together with England succeeded in concluding in Paris military agreements, of which the main object is the acceleration of the revival of German militarism and the inclusion of the Federal German Republic in the military bloc of the Western powers. In October, 1954, a friendship, trade, and navigation agreement was signed between the USA and the Federal Republic. The Federal Republic became a part of the West European Union and was accepted as a member of the North Atlantic Treaty Organization. In December, 1954, the Council of the North Atlantic bloc passed a resolution for preparation for an atomic war.

The "Cold War" and armaments race provoked the increasing resistance by peoples of the entire world. An attempt to ease the tension in international relations gained strength in wide circles of the American people.

In the beginning of 1955 an appeal was made to the government on the part of church organizations, pacifist groups, trade-union, farmer, and youth organizations, student organizations, Negro, women's and other organizations, as well as from individual Americans, urging it to negotiate with the USSR. Some representatives of business and political circles in the USA also spoke in favor of the idea of talks. In May, 1955,

the president of an American company, the National Steel Corporation, E. Weir, announced that "if the threat of war is eliminated, the hostility between Russia and the USA could turn into peaceful competition between two completely different political and social systems" (quoted from the St. Louis *Post-Dispatch*, May 25, 1955). In July, 1955, a group of twenty-nine members of the House of Representatives belonging to the Democratic Party spoke out in favor of talks among the big powers. In a similar letter at the same time, ten members of the House of Representatives belonging to the Republican Party appealed to President Eisenhower. Under the conditions of strengthening the peace movement in all countries, including the USA, the United States took part in a number of international actions which promoted the easing of international tension.[48]

In May, 1955, after the basis was laid as a result of the talks between the government delegations of the USSR and Austria for the solution of the Austrian question, the USA and other powers signed an official agreement for the revival of an independent and democratic Austria.

The government delegation of the USA, headed by President Eisenhower, participated in a meeting of the Heads of State of four powers—the USSR, the USA, England, and France—in Geneva in July, 1955. The meeting had a positive significance in easing tensions in international relations. (Geneva Conference, 1955, q.v.). The American public regarded the USA visit of a Soviet delegation in 1955 and the journey of an American delegation to the USSR with approval. The "Spirit of Geneva" and the attempt at further lessening of international tensions received the support of wide sections of the American people. The convention of independent united trade unions of electrical and radio workers, the annual

---

[48] It is noteworthy that this final section stresses, not American Communist Party desire for an adjustment with the Soviet Union, but the broad American base for an agreement as to coexistence.

convention of AFL trade unions of Illinois, the convention of AFL trade unions of California, of the garment industry trade unions of the AFL, the Electrical Workers of the CIO, and others taking place after the Geneva Conference, spoke up in favor of talks between the governments to end the "Cold War." The National Union of Farmers, the executive committee of the CIO, the National Council of the Churches of Christ, and other organizations came forward in support of the talks. Together with this, influential circles of the USA continued a policy directed against international co-operation. The drawing of countries of the Near and Middle East into military alliances organized under the control of England and the USA and, particularly in the Baghdad Pact, directed against the Soviet Union and other peace-loving governments, continued even after the Geneva Conference of Heads of State of the Four Powers.

At the Geneva Conference of Foreign Ministers of the Four Powers which took place from October 27 to November 16, 1955, the USA, England, and France held a position which hindered the attainment of an agreement on a number of the most important international problems. However, the conference helped to attract the attention of wide circles to the most urgent international problems and helped to make clearer both the difficulties and the possibilities which there are in the successful resolution of international questions.

Now, after the conference, several influential circles in the USA are seeking as before to follow a policy "from a position of strength" to continue the "Cold War." At the same time, a number of well-known figures in the USA are speaking out for peaceful co-operation between the East and the West. Thus, in February, 1956, nearly 100 prominent American scientists, churchmen, political, and trade-union figures appealed to members of the USA Congress "to accept the challenge of peaceful competition" and to remove the obstacles in the way of the development of trade and of delegation exchanges between capitalist and socialist countries.

Wide masses of the American people seeking—as are other peoples of other countries—a lasting peace and the easing of international tension are more and more actively supporting peaceful coexistence of countries with differing socio-economic systems.

BIBLIOGRAPHY

Titles in English Cited as Sources in the Bolshaia Section on United States History

DOCUMENTARY MATERIALS

American State Papers, Vols. 1–38. Washington, 1832–1861.

Annals of the Congress of the United States, Debates and Proceedings . . ., compiled by Joseph Gales, Vols. 1–42, (1789–1824). Washington, 1834–1856.

Aptheker, Herbert, ed. *A Documentary History of the Negro People in the United States.* New York, 1951.

Beloff, Max, ed. *The Debate on the American Revolution, 1761–1783.* London, 1949.

Commager, Henry Steele, ed. *Documents of American History.* New York, 1948.

Commons, John R., ed. *A Documentary History of American Industrial Society*, Vols. 1–10. Cleveland, 1910.

Debs, Eugene Victor. *Speeches of Eugene V. Debs with a Critical Introduction.* New York, 1928.

Foner, Philip Sheldon. *Life and Writings of Frederick Douglass*, Vols. 1–4. New York, 1950–1955.

Franklin, Benjamin. *The Complete Works of Benjamin Franklin*, Vols. 1–10. New York, London, 1887–1888.

Jefferson, Thomas. *The Writings of Thomas Jefferson*, edited by Andrew A. Lipscomb and A. E. Bergh, Vols. 1–20. Washington, 1903–1904.

Lincoln, Abraham. *The Writings of Abraham Lincoln*, Vols. 1–8. Washington, 1905–1906.

Marx, Karl and Engels, Fredrich. *Letters to Americans, 1848–1895.* New York, 1953.

Miller, Hunter, ed. *Treaties and other International Acts of the United States of America*, Vols. 1–8. Washington, 1931–1948.

Paine, Thomas. *The Complete Writings of Thomas Paine*, edited by Philip S. Foner, Vols. 1 and 2. New York, 1945.

Richardson, James Daniel, ed. *A Compilation of the Messages and Papers of the Presidents, 1789–1897*, Vols. 1–10. Washington, 1896–1899.

The Federalist on the New Constitution. Papers by Alexander Hamilton, James Madison, and John Jay. New York, 1945.

United States, Congress. *Congressional Record*, Vols. 1–86. Washington, 1874–1941.

———. *The Congressional Globe*, containing the debates and proceedings. Washington, 1833–1873.

United States, State Department. *Foreign Relations of the United States, 1861–1938.* Washington, 1862–1955.

———. *Treaties, Conventions, International Acts, Protocols, and Agreements Between the United States of America and Other Powers*, Vols. 1–4. Washington, 1910–1938.

Washington, George. *The Writings of George Washington*, Vols. 1–39. Washington, 1931–1944.

SECONDARY STUDIES

Adams, Henry. *History of the United States of America*, Vols. 1–9. New York, 1909–1911.

Allen, James Stewart. *Reconstruction; the Battle for Democracy (1865–1876).* New York, 1937.

Andrews, Charles McLean. *The Colonial Period of American History*, Vols. 1–4. New Haven, 1934–1938, 1947.

Aptheker, Herbert. *American Negro Slave Revolts.* New York, 1944.

———. *Essays in the History of the American Negro.* New York, 1945.

———. *The Labor Movement in the South During Slavery.* New York, 1955.

Bancroft, George. *History of the United States,* Vols. 1–10. Boston, 1857–1874.

Beard, Charles. *Contemporary American History, 1877–1913.* New York, 1914.

Channing, Edward. *A History of the United States,* Vols. 1–6. New York, 1922–1932.

Clark, Dan Elbert. *The West in American History.* New York, 1937.

Commons, John Rogers, *et al. History of Labor in the United States.* New York, 1921.

DuBois, William Edward. *Black Folk: Then and Now.* New York, 1939.

———. *Black Reconstruction.* New York, 1935.

Faulkner, H. U. *American Economic History.* New York, London, 1926.

Foster, William Z. *American Trade Unionism; Principles and Organization, Strategy and Tactics.* New York, 1947.

———. *History of the Communist Party in the United States.* Cleveland, 1952.

Handlin, Oscar, *et al.* eds. *Harvard Guide to American History.* Cambridge, 1954.

Hardy, Jack. *The First American Revolution.* New York, 1937.

Hart, A. B., ed. *The American Nation, A History from Original Sources,* Vols. 1–28. New York, London, 1904–1918.

Hesseltine, William Best. *A History of the South, 1607–1936.* New York, 1936.

Hicks, John Donald. *The Populist Revolt; A History of the Farmer's Alliance and the People's Party.* Minneapolis, 1931.

Hildreth, Richard. *The History of the United States of America,* Vols. 1–6. New York, 1874–1878.

Kirkland, E. C. *A History of American Economic Life.* New York, 1932.

Latane, John H., and Wainhouse, David W. *A History of American Foreign Policy, 1869–1932.* New York, 1940.

Lewis, Edward R. *A History of American Political Thought from the Civil War to the World War.* New York, 1937.

Lippincott, Isaac. *Economic Development of the United States.* New York, London, 1933.

McMaster, John B. *A History of the People of the United States, from the Revolution to the Civil War,* Vols. 1–8. New York, London, 1917–1921.

Milton, George Fort. *Conflict; the American Civil War.* New York, 1941.

Obermann, Karl. *Joseph Weydemeyer, Pioneer of American Socialism.* New York, 1947.

Oneal, James. *The Workers in American History.* New York, 1921.

Parkes, Henry B. *The United States of America, A History.* New York, 1953.

Rhodes, James Ford. *History of the United States from the Compromise of 1850 to the End of the Roosevelt Administration,* Vols. 1–9. New York, 1928.

Rippy, James Fred. *Rivalry of the United States and Great Britain Over Latin America, (1808–1830).* Baltimore, 1929.

Rochester, Anna. *Rulers of America; A Study of Financial Capital.* New York, 1936.

———. *The Populist Movement in the United States.* New York, 1943.

Schlesinger, Arthur. *Political and Social Growth of the American People, 1865–1940.* New York, 1941.

———. *The Age of Jackson.* Boston, 1946.

Schluter, Herman. *Lincoln, Labor, and Slavery.* New York, 1914.

Simons, A. M. *Social Forces in American History.* New York, 1926.

Todes, Charlotte. *William H. Sylvis and the National Labor Union.* New York, 1942.

Turner, Frederick Jackson. *The Frontier in American History.* New York, 1931.

Whitman, Alden. *Labor Parties, 1827–34.* New York, 1943.